THE BRITISH ARMY IN GERMANY (BAOR AND AFTER): AN ORGANIZATIONAL HISTORY, 1947—2004

Graham E. Watson and Richard A. Rinaldi

TIGER LILY PUBLICATIONS LLC

FOR

ORBAT.COM

2005

ISBN 0-9720296-9-9

Table of Contents

ii

Preface

This project began as a simple organizational history of British Army of the Rhine (BAOR), including some information on related British commitments to NATO, and possible reinforcements for BAOR. It then expanded to include detailed orders of battle for BAOR. Finally, the scope widened to include British troops in Berlin and the period following disbanding of BAOR in 1994 as well.

In this work, Dr Watson had primary responsibility for the detailed orders of battle while Mr Rinaldi had primary responsibility for the narrative sections, as well as the overall organization of the work. This was a trans-Atlantic effort over an extended period of time by e-mail and letter, with Dr Watson in Wales and Mr Rinaldi in the US. The book grew slowly over time as information came to the US from Wales and drafts went from the US back to Wales.

A key resource for the order of battle material was the information collected by Dr Watson over the years on the location of armoured, infantry, artillery, engineer and other units of the British Army, as well as various notes on the organization of the British Army during different time periods.[1] However, as the project went on this was supplemented by information generously provided by others. As Dr Watson expressed it in a February 2005 letter, "I owe a great debt to Geoff Fletcher, and his colleague Dave Leftwich, for allowing me access to Dave's extensive files on BAOR. Equally, both Mike Cox and Ewen Bayley directed me towards new material which is included also." Clearly, both authors are extremely grateful for "the valuable contributions of Geoff, Dave, Mike and Ewen." Gentlemen, please accept out thanks for your help.

---

[1] By sheer good fortune, Dr Watson was also completing (with Cliff Lord) the official history of the Royal Corps of Signals while this effort was underway. Research in the archives on signals units also uncovered information on formations to which they were associated or assigned.

Introduction

The BAOR of 1945—like its largely forgotten 1919 namesake—began as an army of occupation in a defeated Germany. However, with the Cold War and NATO it evolved into something quite different. Until then, the British Army had been used to gain and garrison the Empire, and only went onto the continent of Europe in wartime as expeditionary forces. These could indeed grow quite large (the BEF of 1914—1918 or 21st Army Group) but they were still expeditionary forces. When war ended, the Army demobilized and the Regulars returned to their former tasks in the Empire and at home. That did not happen after 1945.

Especially with rearmament and the expansion in 1950—1952, BAOR evolved into a major military force permanently stationed on the continent. This included not only the soldiers, but their wives and children as well. The north German plain became the regular garrison homes for much of the British Army, with "little Englands" scattered about. Especially as the Army shrank and the government ended its "East of Suez" roles, BAOR came to form a significant part of the Army and the major overseas posting for soldiers. Units and personnel could spend years there, so that at least for a some, Germany would come to feel more "home" than did the United Kingdom.[2] Even when BAOR itself was disbanded in 1994, the British Army did not come back from Germany. Now reduced to just two operational divisions, one is in the United Kingdom and the other remains in Germany.

This work is a study of that unique force, a permanent British Army presence on the continent of Europe.

Each section begins with an overview, especially of divisions and brigades, and then continues with one or more detailed orders of battle for the period. These orbats are divided to coincide with major changes in the structure of the forces in Germany. The level of detail of support units tends to increase as we reach more recent times, although all orbats contain details on infantry, armour, artillery, engineers and signals. In the case of artillery, the batteries assigned to a regiment as well as the weapons types are indicated; engineer units are carried down to squadron level.

---

[2] Roy Bainton's *The Long Patrol* is a fascinating look at this experience, based mainly on interviews with service personnel, their wives, and children. In his overview of British Army officership, Patrick Mileham suggests that the permanent stationing on the continent of BAOR "enabled withdrawal from imperial stations during the 1950s to seem more palatable to regular and career officers…." "Fifty Years of British Army Officership 1960—2010, Part I: Retrospective" *Defense & Security Analysis*, Mar 2004 (Vol 20, No 1), 82.

For all units, location is given (or shown as "location unknown"). A replacement unit is always at the same location as its predecessor unless a new location is given for the replacement unit. In the case of artillery, unless indicated otherwise a replacement regiment has the same armament as the unit it replaces and thus weapons types are not repeated.

Two shorthand terms are used for convenience in the detailed orders of battle. First, "arrived" is used in the lists for both units newly arriving in Germany or the post under control of the indicated formation and for units that might have already been at a particular station but simply newly assigned to the formation. Second, the term "disbanded" is used both in its proper sense and as an alternative for "placed in suspended animation." In the latter case, the difference is material for those doing unit lineages but is largely irrelevant for these orders of battle. In some cases, units shown as "left" (i.e., leaving Germany or the particular formation) may actually have been disbanded or placed in suspended animation, although we have made the distinction where we were sure.

The information in this work is as accurate as possible. However, in some areas information is imperfect or even contradictory; some discrepancies are noted in the text or details. Where required, the authors have made their best determination based on the information available. Our details are far better because of the help provided by others, but the authors alone are responsible for any errors that might remain.

Garrison Force

On 25 Aug 1945, 21st Army Group became British Army of the Rhine, using the designation of the post-World War I occupation force, which actually had been concentrated along the Rhine. The original BAOR remained in Germany for 10 years, but from 1920 until it departed in 1929 it was little more than a weak division serving on occupation duties.[3]

The second and better-known BAOR also began as an occupation force, although its area extended well beyond the Rhine into northwest Germany. Initially with three corps districts (I, VIII and XXX) and several divisions, most of the wartime units were demobilized during 1946. The VIII and XXX Corps Districts were disbanded in 1946 and the I Corps District in Jun 1947. By Jan 1947, BAOR was reduced to three divisions: 7th Armoured, 5th Infantry, and 53rd (Welsh) Infantry.[4] The period of demobilization (1946—1947) is detailed below, beginning on page 7.

On 1 Feb 1947 the 2nd Infantry Division was reformed from what had been 53rd (Welsh) Infantry Division. 5th Infantry Division was disbanded in Sep 1947, although its brigades lingered to Mar 1948. 7th Armoured Division was gradually merged into Hannover District during 1947 and then disbanded later the same year.[5] In Feb 1948 the 2nd Parachute Brigade moved from England to BAOR; it would be renumbered there as 16th, forming the only active parachute brigade in the British Army.[6]

From Apr 1948 HQ BAOR was at Bad Oeynhausen. The two main administrative components were Hamburg District and Hannover District. A Rhine District had existed until Apr 1947, at which point it became headquarters for Rhine Army Troops. The main supply headquarters was at Düsseldorf, and there was a communications zone headquarters at Emblem in Belgium.

---

[3] A brief overview of the first BAOR is contained below in the Appendix.
[4] The last had officially become 'X' Division in Jul 1946, with its three brigades coming from it and the 51st and 52nd Divisions. However, it seems that it was still commonly called by its old designation and so referred to in published sources.
[5].The formal disbanding may have occurred in early 1948. During its existence, the district was "Hannover" (the English spelling of the city), although the German spelling "Hanover" has now become common even in English.
[6] It is not clear what operational role (if any) might have been intended for the brigade. Its battalions were widely scattered, and the one in Lübeck was only 4-6 miles from the Soviet Zone.

Map: The North German Plain
BAOR was scattered throughout much of this area

This was a garrison force, distributed in various posts—formerly housing the German Army—across north-west Germany.[7] In Jan 1948 the British forces in Germany totaled 11 armoured regiments and 14 infantry battalions (exclusive of those in Berlin). This changed by the following year to eight armoured regiments and 16 infantry battalions; three of the latter were parachute; these last moved to England in Oct 1949 when 16th Parachute Brigade Group was shifted to Aldershot. 7th Armoured Division reformed in 1949. However, both it and 2nd Infantry Division also served as district headquarters. The divisions

---

[7] Ironically, according to those interviewed by Bainton (*The Long Patrol*), the German barracks were often superior to those available at the time in the United Kingdom.

and districts were separated in 1950, returning the former to a purely tactical role.[8]

2nd Infantry Division had its traditional components, the 4th Infantry, 5th Infantry and 6th Infantry Brigades. 7th Armoured Division had 7th Armoured and 31st Lorried Infantry Brigades.[9] Other than division artillery, there was but a single medium regiment and a locating regiment in the command. BAOR had limited supporting units other than those found in the two division/districts.

One lingering aspect of BAOR's creation as a garrison force is that its units were scattered in a number of locations and not always co-located with other elements of their assigned brigade or division. This remained true throughout BAOR's existence. Division headquarters were fairly stable in location, but brigade headquarters were shifted among the garrisons from time to time. A list of the principal garrison cities in Germany, with associated formation headquarters, is contained below at page 145.

Beginning in 1949 BAOR began limited patrolling of the border with East Germany, but their efforts never matched those of the US Army, with the US Constabulary and then its armored cavalry regiments dedicated to the task. By 1950, important villages within three kilometers of the border were to be visited fortnightly.[10]

A detailed order of battle for BAOR 1948—1950 begins on page 13.

---

[8] Rhine District seems to have reappeared by 1952, along with a new Lubbecke District. By 1957, only the Hannover and Rhine Districts were still in existence. By 1960 the former was gone although a Rhine Area was present. It seems to have disappeared by 1965.

[9] 7th Armoured Division ended World War II with 22nd Armoured and 131st Infantry Brigades; these were both Territorial Army formations and their designations reverted to the TA Jan 1947. 7th Armoured Brigade had been an original component of the division, although later separated and serving as an independent brigade for most of the war. The number "31" had no prior connection with motorized units or the division; the wartime 31st Infantry Brigade became 1st Airlanding Brigade in 1941, and the number was used again briefly in 1946 by the former 6th Airlanding Brigade in Palestine.

[10] This activity would grow by 1964 to patrols once a week in the intended operations zone of BAOR; this was primarily symbolic and for training rather than serious border patrol (which the British considered a German responsibility). This effort was further reduced to token patrols once a month by 1970. The frequency later increased in the 1980s, but the patrols (9-31 men) were not issued ammunition. See Appendix I (British Border Operations in Germany) in William E. Stacy, *US Army Border Operations in Germany, 1945—1983* (HQ, US Army Europe and 7th Army, 1984).

▭ *Demobilization 1946—1947*

A few formation ending the war with 21st Army Group left during 1945. XII Corps was disbanded May 1945; 3rd Infantry Division left for Palestine Nov 1945; 6th Airborne Division went to the UK May 1945 (and then to Palestine); 79th Armoured Division and its brigades, along with 34th Armoured Brigade and 1st Armoured Engineer Brigade were all disbanded in 1945. Headquarters Second Army survived to Jun 1946 when it was disbanded. 11th Armoured Division was disbanded Feb 1946.

BAOR 11 Mar 1946

I Corps District (states of Rhineland and Westphalia)

Guards Division
     5th Guards Brigade
     6th Guards Brigade
     32nd Guards Brigade
49th (West Riding) Infantry Division
     56th Infantry Brigade
     146th Infantry Brigade
     147th Infantry Brigade
52nd (Lowland) Infantry Division
     155th Infantry Brigade
     156th Infantry Brigade
     157th Infantry Brigade
53rd (Welsh) Infantry Division
     71st Infantry Brigade
     158th Infantry Brigade
     159th Infantry Brigade <ex 11th Armoured Division>
     160th Infantry Brigade

VIII Corps District (state of Schleswig-Holstein)

4th Armoured Brigade
Jewish Infantry Brigade Group
7th Armoured Division
     22nd Armoured Brigade
     131st Infantry Brigade <detached to Berlin>
     13th Infantry Brigade <attached, from 5th Infantry Division>

15th

15th (Scottish) Infantry Division[11]
    46th Infantry Brigade

XXX Corps District (state of Hannover)

8th Armoured Brigade [HQ only]
5th Infantry Division
    15th Infantry Brigade
    17th Infantry Brigade
43rd (Wessex) Infantry Division
    129th Infantry Brigade
    130th Infantry Brigade
    214th Infantry Brigade
51st (Highland) Infantry Division
    152nd Infantry Brigade
    153rd Infantry Brigade
    154th Infantry Brigade
3rd Canadian Division, CAOF[12]
    2nd/7th Canadian Infantry Brigade
    2nd/8th Canadian Infantry Brigade
    2nd/9th Canadian Infantry Brigade

Changes During 1946

VIII Corps District was disbanded Apr 1946 and XXX Corps District was disbanded Sep 1946.

Guards Division was disbanded Dec 1946; 5th Guards Brigade went to Berlin Aug 1946, 6th Guards Brigade transferred to Hamburg District, and 32nd Guards Brigade also came under Hamburg District in Jun 1946 (and was disbanded Dec 1946).

15th (Scottish) Infantry Division and its last brigade (46th) were disbanded in Apr 1946.

43rd (Wessex) Infantry Division was disbanded Aug 1946. Its 130th Infantry Brigade went to Berlin Jun 1946, then was assigned to 5th Infantry Division Aug-Dec 1946 before disbanding. The other two brigades survived the

[11] The division's 227th Infantry Brigade was disbanded Jan 1946 and 44th Infantry Brigade in Feb 1946.
[12] Canadian Army Occupation Force. This was technically a new formation, taking over its units 15 Jun 1945, and not the wartime 3rd Canadian Infantry Division.

division, with 214th Infantry Brigade disbanded Oct 1946 and 129th Infantry Brigade in Nov 1946.

49th (West Riding) Infantry Division and its 56th and 147th Infantry Brigades were all disbanded Oct 1946; 146th Infantry Brigade had been disbanded in Aug 1946.

51st (Highland) Infantry Division and its 152nd Infantry Brigade were disbanded Aug 1946; 154th Infantry Brigade had been disbanded in Jun 1946; and 153rd Infantry Brigade went to 53rd (Welsh) Infantry Division Aug 1946.

52nd (Lowland) Infantry Division and its 156th Infantry Brigade were disbanded in Aug 1946; its 155th Infantry Brigade had been disbanded the month before; its 157th Infantry Brigade went to 53rd (Welsh) Infantry Division Aug 1946.

3rd Canadian Division, CAOF, began to draw down the end of Mar 1946 and was withdrawn in stages over the next three months; its headquarters turned over its area of responsibility on 15 May 1946 and was disbanded 20 Jun 1946.

8th Armoured Brigade (reduced to its HQ only) was disbanded in Mar 1946.

BAOR 2 Jan 1947

Hamburg District
2nd Bn Welsh Guards
2nd Bn Seaforth Highlanders [due to move to the UK]
4th Armoured Brigade
       Royal Scots Greys
       7th Hussars
       2nd Royal Tank Regt
Hamburg Sub Area
       2nd Bn Irish Gds
       2nd Bn Rifle Brigade [arriving]
Schleswig-Holstein Sub Area[13]
       10th Hussars
       3rd Royal Tank Regt
       21st Field Regt RA
       29th Field Regt RA
       1st Heavy Regt RA
       153rd LAA Regt RA
       1st Bn Middlesex Regt [MG]

---

[13] Formed from HQ Guards Division.

I Corps District

Royal Horse Guards
40th Garrison (Hannover)
41st Garrison (Cologne)
42nd Garrison (Brussels)

7th Armoured Division
11th Hussars
7th Armoured Brigade
       5th R Inniskilling Dragoon Gds
       8th Hussars
       1st Royal Tank Regt
       5th Royal Tank Regt
       1st Bn Rifle Brigade
31st Infantry Brigade
       1st Bn Royal Norfolk Regt
       1st Bn Leicester Regt
       1st Bn Sherwood Foresters
       1st Bn KO Yorkshire LI
3rd Regt RHA
5th Regt RHA
4th Regt RHA [atk]
2nd Light AA Regt RA

5th Infantry Division
Royal Dragoons
13th/18th Hussars
15th Infantry Brigade
       2nd Bn Devonshire Regt
       1st Bn York and Lancaster Regt
17th Infantry Brigade
       2nd Bn South Staffords Regt
       1st Bn Dorset Regt
       2nd Bn Northamptonshire Regt
30th Infantry Brigade
       1st Bn Royal Berkshire Regt
       2nd Bn Wiltshire Regt
1st Bn Manchester Regt [MG; leaving for the UK]
25th Field Regt RA
26th Field Regt RA

[5th Infantry Division]
32nd Field Regt RA
24th Atk Regt RA
5th Light AA Regt RA

53rd (Welsh) Infantry Division[14]
14th/20th Hussars
153rd Infantry Brigade
     1st Bn Black Watch
     1st Bn Gordon Highlanders
     1st Bn Royal Fusiliers
157th Infantry Brigade
     2nd Bn Royal Scots Fusiliers
160th Infantry Brigade
     2nd Bn Grenadier Gds
     1st Bn Royal Welch Fusiliers
     1st Bn East Lancashire Regt
1st Bn Cheshire Regt [MG]
69th Field Regt RA
76th Field Regt RA
3rd Medium Regt R A
7th Medium Regt RA
55th Atk Regt RA

Changes During 1947

I Corps District was disbanded Jun 1947.

7th Armoured Division merged with Hannover District during 1947. It was effectively disbanded in this process, but seems to have lingered until an official disbanding in early 1948. Its wartime 22nd Armoured and 131st Infantry Brigades were renumbered in Jan 1947 as 7th Armoured and 31st Infantry.

5th Infantry Division was disbanded Sep 1947. Its 13th, 15th and 17th Infantry Brigades all survived into 1948. Its 30th (or 130th?) Infantry Brigade, formed in Aug 1946, was disbanded in Aug 1947.

53rd Infantry Division—technically 'X' Division—was renumbered Feb 1947 as 2nd Infantry Division. Its 158th Infantry Brigade had been disbanded in Jul

---

[14] Officially, 'X' Division from Jul 1946 and reorganized with a brigade each from the 51st, 52nd and 53rd Divisions, but apparently still generally referred to as the 53rd Infantry Division.

1946 and replaced by 153rd Infantry Brigade. (159th Infantry Brigade, returned to the division after wartime service with 11th Armoured Division, was also disbanded in Jul 1946.) The 153rd, 157th and 160th Infantry Brigades became the 6th, 5th and 4th Infantry Brigades, respectively, when the division was renumbered.

On formation, 2nd Infantry Division (HQ Hilden) was organized as follows:
14th/20th Hussars, replaced during 1947 by 10th Hussars
Royal Horse Guards assigned by Aug 1947 until sometime later in the year
1st Bn Cheshire Regt [MG], replaced ca. Feb 1947 by 1st Bn Middlesex Regt
4th Infantry Brigade (HQ Hubblerath)
       1st Bn Royal Welch Fusiliers
       1st Bn East Lancashire Regt
       2nd Bn Grenadier Gds
5th Infantry Brigade (HQ Dortmund; Sep 1947 to Iserlohn)
       1st Bn Royal Fusiliers
       2nd Bn Royal Scots Fusiliers
       2nd Bn Queen's Regt [added by Aug 1947]
6th Infantry Brigade (HQ Munster)
       1st Bn Black Watch
       1st Bn Gordon Highlanders
       2nd Bn Wiltshire Regt
29th Field Regt RA <renumbered Apr 1947 as 19th>
69th Field Regt RA <renumbered Apr 1947 as 40th>
76th Field Regt RA <renumbered Apr 1947 as 42nd>
3rd Medium Regt RA <renumbered Apr 1947 as 15th; became Corps Troops>
7th Medium Regt RA <renumbered Apr 1947 as 32nd; returned to UK 1947>
55th Atk Regt RA <renumbered Apr 1947 as 53rd>
22nd Light AA Regt RA [joined Apr 1947]

▨ *BAOR 1948—1950*

HQ BAOR	*Bad Oyenhausen*
HQ BAOR Signal Regt	*Bad Oyenhausen*
11th Air Formation Signal Regt	*Buckeburg (Lemgo?)*
1st Wireless Regt	*Gluckstadt (Munster?)*
2nd LoC Signal Regt	*Hamburg; to Düsseldorf* 1950
29 Army Troops RE	*location unknown* [to the UK Mar 1948]

  562, 564, 565 Fd Sqns and 563 Fd Pk Sqn RE

30 Army Troops RE   *location unknown* [to the UK Jan 1949]

  57, 61, 66 Fd Sqns and 20 Fd Pk Sqn RE

3 Railway Operating Group RE[15]   *location unknown*

  253, 254, 348 Railway Sqns RE

14 Field Survey Sqn RE   *Mönchen-Gladbach*

HQ 5th AGRA (AA) [formed Nov 1950]   *Delmenhorst*

⊠ **2nd Infantry Division**

HQ 2nd Infantry Division	*Hilden*
2nd Infantry Division Signal Regt	*Hilden*
Royal Horse Gds	*Wolfenbüttel* [left 1948]
10th Hussars [div recce]	*Iserlohn*
3rd Hussars [joined 1949]	*location unknown*
19th Field Regt RA	*Düsseldorf*

  25, 28, 67 Field Btys RA [25pdr]

40th Field Regt RA   *Dortmund*

  78, 109, 129 Field Btys RA [25pdr]

42nd Field Regt RA   *Essen*

  68, 87, 159 Field Btys RA [25pdr]

53rd Atk Regt RA   *location unknown* [disbanded Sep 1948]

  106th, 110th, 115th, 205th Atk Btys RA

10th Atk Regt RA[16] [arrived Sep 1948] *Detmold*

  Q, X, Y, Z Atk Btys RA [17pdr]

22nd Light AA Regt   *Menden*

  47, 48, 53 LAA Btys RA [40mm]

---

[15] Disbanded ca. 1951 (no later than 1952). A 2 Railway Construction and Maintenance Group was in Germany until disbanded Mar 1948.

[16] Converted Nov 1950 to a field regiment RA. Q, X and Y became field batteries while Z became a light mortar battery.

[2nd Infantry Division]
23 Field Engineer Regt[17]   *Hameln* ;1949 to *Dortmund*
        2, 5, 38 Field Sqns and 21 Field Pk Sqn RE

HQ 4th INFANTRY BRIGADE[18]   *Hubblerath*
2nd Bn Grenadier Gds   *Krefeld*
        replaced May 1949 by 1st Bn Wiltshire Regt
        replaced Apr 1950 by 1st Bn Welsh Gds at *Hubblerath*
1st Bn Royal Welch Fusiliers   *Hubblerath*
        replaced May 1949 by 1st Bn Royal Norfolk Regt
1st Bn York and Lancaster Regt   *Krefeld*
        replaced 1948 by 1st Bn Manchester Regt
        replaced Sep 1950 by 2nd Bn Grenadier Gds

HQ 5th INFANTRY BRIGADE   *Iserlohn*
1st Bn Royal Fusiliers   *Iserlohn*
        replaced Dec 1949 by 1st Bn Queen's Regt
2nd Bn Queen's Regt   *Dortmund*
        replaced sep 1948 by 1st Bn Durham LI
2nd Bn Royal Scots Fusiliers   *Iserlohn*
        replaced Oct 1948 by 1st Bn King's (Liverpool) Regt
1st Bn Middlesex Regt   *location unknown* [left 1948]

HQ 6th INFANTRY BRIGADE   *Munster*
1st Bn Black Watch   *Duisburg*
1st Bn Gordon Highlanders   *Essen*
        replaced May 1949 by 1st Bn Worcestershire Regt
2nd Bn Wiltshire Regt   *Bielefeld*
        renumbered 1st Bn of regt Nov 1948
        replaced Feb 1949 by 1st Bn Royal Scots Fusiliers
2nd Bn Grenadier Gds [arrived May 1949]   *location unknown* [left
        Sep 1950]

---

[17] Designated 2nd Division RE to 1948.
[18] The brigade may have been redesignated as Guards Sep 1950 when two battalions came from the Foot Guards; the redesignation would have occurred no later than Feb 1951 when all three battalions were Guards.

⊡ [Hannover District] 7th Armoured Division[19]

HQ 7th Armoured Division [reformed Mar 1949]   *Verden*

7th Armoured Division Signal Regt [reformed Mar 1949]   *Verden*

Royal Dragoons   *Lubbecke*

Royal Horse Guards [joined 1948]   *Wolfenbüttel*?

11th Hussars [recce]   *Wesendorf*

7th Hussars [div atk] [joined 1950]   *Hohne*

2nd Bn Grenadier Gds [leader training unit]   *location unknown*[left May
          1949]

3rd Field Regt RHA   *Munsterlager*
          D, J, M Btys RHA [Sexton]

4th Field Regt RHA   *Hohne*
          F, N, V Btys RHA [Sexton]

2nd Field Regt RHA [joined 1950]   *Hildesheim*
          H, I, L Btys RHA [Sexton]

10th Atk Regt RA   *Detmold*? [left Sep 1948]
          Q, X, Y, Z Atk Btys RA [17pdr]

49th Atk Regt RA   *location unknown* [left 1948]
          55, 127, 143, 170 Atk Btys RA

12th LAA Regt RA   *Celle*
          T, 9, 34 LAA Btys RA [40mm]

21 Field Engineer Regt [formed Dec 1949]   *Hameln*; later *Nienburg*]
          4, 7, 27 Field Sqns and 45 Field Pk Sqn RE

HQ 7th ARMOURED BRIGADE   *Soltau*

5th Royal Inniskilling Dgn Gds   *Paderborn* [see Note 1 below]

Royal Scots Greys   *Luneburg* [left Nov 1948]

8th Hussars   *location unknown*

1st Royal Tank Regt   *Detmold* [see Note 1 below]

5th Royal Tank Regt   *Hohne*

1st Bn Rifle Brigade   *Minden*

HQ 15th INFANTRY BRIGADE   *location unknown* [disbanded Mar 1948][20]

1st Bn Dorset Regt

1st Bn Wiltshire Regt

---

[19] 7th Armoured Division reformed beginning Mar 1949. Unless otherwise indicated,
units and formations shown were under Hannover District until that date.

[20] HQ 15th and 17th Infantry Brigades were disbanded Mar 1948 at Hanover (the latter's
last battalion left Feb 1948). HQ 13th Infantry Brigade surrendered its last battalion
Mar 1948 and was disbanded as well. All were left over from 5th Infantry Division.

HQ 31ˢᵗ LORRIED INFANTRY BRIGADE[21]   *Osnabrück*
1ˢᵗ Bn Sherwood Foresters [arrived Mar 1948]   *Goslar*
1ˢᵗ Bn Oxford and Bucks LI [arrived Jul 1948]   *location unknown*
        replaced May 1949 by 1ˢᵗ Bn Worcestershire Regt
1ˢᵗ Bn East Yorkshire Regt [arrived 1950?]   *Luneburg*
1ˢᵗ Bn York & Lancaster Regt [arrived Sep 1950]   *Brunswick*

Hamburg District

3ʳᵈ Hussars [joined 1948]   *location unknown* [left 1949]
15ᵗʰ/19ᵗʰ Hussars [arrived Oct 1949]   *Lubbecke*
1ˢᵗ Bn York and Lancaster Regt [joined 1949 ex Hamburg Sub Area]
29ᵗʰ Field Regt RA [joined 1948 ex 4ᵗʰ AGRA]

Hamburg Sub Area [disbanded 1949]
        1ˢᵗ Bn Sherwood Foresters [left 1948]
        1ˢᵗ Bn York & Lancaster Regt [arrived 1948; District Troops 1949]]

Schleswig-Holstein Sub Area [disbanded 1948]
        10ᵗʰ Hussars
        3ʳᵈ Royal Tank Regt [to the UK 1948]

HQ 4ᵀᴴ ARMOURED BRIGADE   *location unknown* [disbanded early 1948]
2ⁿᵈ Royal Tank Regt
1ˢᵗ Bn Worcestershire Regt
1ˢᵗ Bn Oxford and Bucks LI

HQ 4ᵗʰ AGRA (Field)[22]   *Hamburg?*
29ᵗʰ Field Regt RA [training]   *location unknown* [District Troops 1948]
        8, 79, 145 Field Btys RA
15ᵗʰ Medium Regt RA   *Lippstadt*
        7, 38 Med Btys RA [5.5"]
94ᵗʰ Observation Regt RA   *Luneburg*
        210, 211 Loc Btys RA

---

[21] Infantry Brigade or Independent Infantry Brigade until ca. Mar 1949. The brigade's battalions were posted away between Apr 1947 and Jan 1948 and then it was reformed.
[22] Formed 1947 from HQ RA Hamburg District. Used to form HQ CRA 7ᵗʰ Armoured Division Apr 1950.

⊠ **16th Parachute Brigade**[23] [arrived Feb 1948]   *location unknown*
        [left Oct 1949]
1st Bn Parachute Regt   *Lubbecke*
2nd Bn Parachute Regt   *Husum*
3rd Bn Parachute Regt   *Itzehe*
Gds Indep Para Coy [pathfinder unit]   *location unknown*
33rd Abn Light Regt RA   *location unknown*
9th Para Sqn RE   *location unknown*

Note 1: 33rd Armoured Brigade—intended for 11th Armoured Division—began forming in Nov 1950; in Feb 1951 its HQ moved to Bad Lippspringe. It initially contained 5th Royal Inniskilling Dragoon Guards (Paderborn, ex 7th Armoured Brigade) and 1st Royal Tank Regt (Detmold, also ex 7th Armoured Brigade). It would also gain the 1st Bn KRRC, although possibly not until 1951.

Note 2: 1 Engineer Training Establishment: formed 1948 at Hameln from 7th Armoured Division RE, with 1, 209, 210 and 211 Field Sqns RE. (1 Field Sqn RE relieved before Oct 1948.) 209, 210 and 211 Field Sqns RE renumbered twice, finally becoming 4, 6 and 45 Field Sqns RE. There was also a 'B' Depot Sqn RE. In Dec 1949 1 Engineer Training Establishment was redesignated 21 Field Engineer Regiment, the divisional regiment for 7th Armoured Division.

---

[23] Designated 2nd Parachute Brigade (4th/6th, 5th and 7th Bns) on arrival; brigade and battalions renumbered Jul 1948.

The 1950s and 1960s: Expansion and Contraction

Organizationally, these two decades may have seen the most changes in BAOR. The period began with rearmament and expansion and ended with an all-volunteer Army and retrenchment. In between, the Army shuffled division designations, reorganized, and replaced World War II era equipment with new tanks and armoured cars, mechanised the infantry with APCs, and gained new artillery weapons including rockets and guided missiles.

Formations

By the end of 1950 British troops were fighting a Communist insurgency in Malaya, part of the conventional war in Korea, and on guard elsewhere in the world as the Cold War appeared to be turning hot. This led to a number of changes in the British Army, as well as increased attention to NATO forces in Germany.[24] A new division (11th Armoured) was formed beginning Sep 1950 in Germany, with 33rd Armoured and 91st Lorried Infantry Brigades.[25] 6th Armoured Division (20th Armoured and 61st Lorried Infantry Brigades) was formed in the UK May 1951 for a strategic reserve role. However, in Mar 1952 it moved to Germany.[26]

As a result of this buildup, 1 British Corps was reformed late 1951, also (like BAOR) at Bad Oyenhausen. In 1953 its HQ moved to Bielefeld. NATO created the Northern Army Group (NORTHAG) on 29 Nov 1952; the C-in-C BAOR was also C-in-C NORTHAG.[27] In wartime, this NATO headquarters

---

[24] Just as the increase in BAOR led to the UK's first major permanent peacetime ground force on the Continent, the US also greatly expanded its forces in Germany (from one division to five) and likewise established its first permanent ground force in Europe. Both countries also expanded their air forces in Germany. By the middle of the 1950s, NATO had a goal of 30 divisions on the central front (Germany): 4 British, 5 US, 12 West German, 2 each Dutch and Belgian and 5 French.

[25] The armoured brigade was actually formed beginning in Nov 1950. The brigade numbers had no prior connection with the division, and the number "91" had not been used for a brigade since the First World War.

[26] The other division formed for the strategic reserve role, 3rd Infantry, would spend most of the 1950s in the Middle East. The result, as will be discussed later, is that there were usually no Regular formations in the UK that could be used to reinforce BAOR. A 20th Armoured Brigade had been part of 6th Armoured Division in World War II, but it was detached before the division saw any service; a 61st Infantry Brigade had formed part of the division towards the end of the war.

[27] NATO established two army groups in Germany: Northern (NORTHAG) and Central (CENTAG). The titles seem a bit overblown, although each did have one

would command the front roughly from Hamburg to Kassel (known informally as the North German Plain). It had, north to south, I Dutch Corps, 1 British Corps, and I Belgian Corps. When West Germany created an army after 1955, its I Army Corps would be added to NORTHAG as well, with a sector to the north of the British. The bulk of Germany, along with the Benelux countries and (until the 1960s) France formed the territory of Allied Forces Central Europe, or AFCENT. Schleswig-Holstein in northern Germany was grouped with Denmark and Norway under Allied Forces Northern Europe, or AFNORTH.

HQ BAOR moved to Rheindahlen near Mönchen Gladbach 4 Oct 1954.[28]

The expanded BAOR was deployed as follows:

2nd Infantry Division	Hilden
4th Guards Brigade[29]	Hubblerath
5th Infantry Brigade	Iserlohn
6th Infantry Brigade	Munster; Dec 1951 Wuppertal
6th Armoured Division	Herford; 1953 to Bunde
20th Armoured Brigade	Munster
61st Lorried Infantry Brigade	Minden
7th Armoured Division	Verden
7th Armoured Brigade	Soltau
31st Lorried Infantry Brigade	Minden; Oct 1951 Luneburg[30]
11th Armoured Division	Herford
33rd Armoured Brigade	Bad Lippspringe
91st Lorried Infantry Brigade	Hildesheim

This marked the high point in strength for BAOR, with four divisions and nine brigades, along with supporting units. The detailed order of battle for this period (1951-Mar 1956) begins below on page 31.

---

subordinate army headquarters: BAOR in NORTHAG and Seventh US Army in CENTAG. The two army commanders were also the designated wartime army group commanders. If NATO went to war, NORTHAG would become the active command headquarters and BAOR would become a support headquarters.

[28] Until recently, this location was almost always shown in published works as Mönchen Gladbach or Mönchengladbach rather than Rheindahlen. HQ Rhine Area (formerly HQ Rhine Army Troops) was still in existence as late as 1959, also located at Rheindahlen.

[29] This may have been officially 4th (Guards) Infantry Brigade, but it was usually called simply 4th Guards Brigade.

[30] The move from Osnabrück to Minden may have been in 1950.

These divisions were not unlike their World War II counterparts in organization, and much of the equipment was of that vintage as well. One difference was that the anti-tank role had shifted in 1950 from the Royal Artillery to the Royal Armoured Corps. The divisional regiment RAC was initially equipped with ex-RA M10 tank destroyers, replaced from 1952 by the Charioteer tank destroyer. Comet tanks from the end of World War II remained in use until replaced by the newer Centurion (the first mark of which itself had appeared in 1945). The Centurion remained in production until 1962, with newer marks gaining larger guns along with other improvements. The Conqueror heavy tank was introduced at the rate of one troop per squadron in 1954—it was the first British tank to mount a 120mm gun, and remained in service into the 1960s.

Infantry still rode in half tracks (the armoured brigade) or trucks (lorried brigades).[31] Artillery had the towed 25-pounder or the Sexton SP 25-pounder. Second-line (B) vehicles were mostly of World War II manufacture.

The official organization (as at Nov 1951) for British divisions was as follows:
ARMOURED DIVISION
      Armoured Brigade (3 armoured regiments, 1 motor battalion)
      Lorried Infantry Brigade (3 infantry battalions)
      Armoured Car Regiment
      Divisional Regiment RAC
      2 Field (SP) Regiments RHA[32]

---

[31] Those battalions in half tracks gradually replaced them with four-wheel drive vehicles and the Humber FV1600 series. (These were APCs built on a one-ton truck chassis and could carry 6-8 men.) Normal infantry battalions could be carried by an RASC platoon of 30 three-ton trucks, but there were not enough of these to have a platoon for each infantry battalion. (The lorried brigades should have had sufficient RASC transport to carry everyone.) There were also two RASC units with de-turreted tanks and old M3 halftracks, allotted to each of the two infantry divisions in 1956. (These were disbanded in 1957.) As late as 1956 only two infantry battalions in BAOR (those in 7th and 20th Armoured Brigades) had some APCs (the Humbers). These were replaced 1957 by the Saracen 6-wheeled APC. The RAC took over this role, with 14th/20th King's Hussars using two squadrons to man APCs and its third in tanks to replace the disbanded independent squadron in Berlin. 4th RTR then took over this role from Nov 1960 to Apr 1963. The infantry (1st Bn Royal Northumberland Fusiliers and 1st Bn Royal Irish Fusiliers at the time) finally took over responsibility for these vehicles and their drivers in Apr 1963. It was only after this that APCs (the new FV432 tracked series) gradually became introduced to the remaining infantry in BAOR. This might have taken until very late in the 1960s.
[32] Some sources indicate that one of these might still have been equipped with towed 25-pounders. The Sextons were retired in the 1950s. However, the regiments in 7th and 20th Armoured Brigades had the US M44 (SP 155mm howitzer) ca. 1958 (and

1 LAA Regiment RA
Locating Battery RA
Field Engineer Regiment
Signal Regiment
OP Flight

INFANTRY DIVISION
Infantry Brigade (3 battalions)
Infantry Brigade (3 battalions)
Infantry Brigade (3 battalions)
Divisional Regiment RAC
3 Field Regiments RA
1 Light Regiment RA
1 LAA Regiment RA
Locating Battery RA
Field Engineer Regiment
Signal Regiment
OP Flight

This meant that BAOR should have had 16 regiments of armour[33] and 21 battalions of infantry in its four divisions. At its peak it numbered around 77,000 personnel.

The first major reorganization occurred 1 Apr 1956 when 11th Armoured Division was converted to 4th Infantry Division. The 4th was formed with the 10th, 11th and 12th Infantry Brigades (the traditional numbers for this division). This was accomplished by taking the lorried brigades from the other two armoured divisions along with the assets of 11th Armoured Division. The result was that the 2nd and 4th Infantry Divisions each had three infantry brigades and each brigade had one armoured regiment and three infantry battalions. The 6th and 7th Armoured Divisions retained only their former armoured brigades; the brigade headquarters were disbanded and these two "divisions" thus became little more than large brigade groups. The theory was that the two infantry divisions would hold the line, and the two armoured divisions would be available as a reserve and counter-attacking force.

---

possibly earlier). This would continue until the new Abbot (a British-produced SP 105mm) was introduced beginning 1965. The last 25-pounder regiment finally disappeared from the Army in 1967.

[33] At this time there were 30 regiments between the Royal Armoured Corps (RAC) and the Household Cavalry, so BAOR (which also had a non-divisional armoured car regiment) had over half of them.

2nd Infantry Division and its three brigades largely remained at their prior locations, although 6th Infantry Brigade shifted from Wuppertal to Munster. The new 4th Infantry Division was established at Herford, the site of 11th Armoured Division HQ. 10th Infantry Brigade (the former 91st Lorried Infantry) remained at Hildesheim. 11th Infantry Brigade (the former 61st Lorried) remained at Minden. 12th Infantry Brigade (the former 31st Lorried Infantry) relocated to Osnabrück from Luneburg. 6th and 7th Armoured Divisions, now without any subordinate brigades, kept their respective headquarters at Bunde and Verden. A new 21st Independent Infantry Brigade appeared, possibly around Mar 1956 (although some sources have shown a date as late as Apr 1957). Established at Osnabrück, the intended purpose of this brigade is not exactly clear.[34]

A detailed order of battle for the period Apr 1956 to Sep 1957 is given below at page 39.

In Apr 1957 the government announced the end of National Service, with no more call-ups after 1960. From that date, the Army would be all volunteers. This would necessitate a large reduction in Army strength and in the number of units. Armour would be cut from 30 regiments to 23 (with 14 allotted to BAOR); infantry battalions (excluding Gurkhas) would fall from 77 to 60. Artillery (especially anti-aircraft) and engineers would also be reduced, along with other supporting arms and various headquarters.

Facing downsizing as part of this change, BAOR began to revise the 1956 organization in Sep 1957. In 2nd Infantry Division, 6th Infantry Brigade shifted from Munster back to Wuppertal. 4th Infantry Division kept the 11th Infantry Brigade at Minden, shifted the 12th Infantry Brigade to Hildesheim, and took under command the 21st Infantry Brigade at Osnabrück.[35] In 6th Armoured Division, the 20th Armoured Brigade HQ was reestablished at Detmold. 7th Armoured Division reformed 7th Armoured Brigade HQ at Soltau, and also took 10th Infantry Brigade (with its HQ now at Luneburg) under command. Artillery regiments and field squadrons RE were tasked for support of particular brigades.

A detailed order of battle for Sep 1957 to Apr 1958 begins below at page 45.

The changes in Sep 1957 proved to be interim, with another reorganization in Apr 1958 as BAOR completed the organizational framework for its reduced

[34] One theory is that it might have been established as a holding unit for battalions in Germany facing amalgamation, although its creation seems early for that role.
[35] In Dec 1957, the 12th Infantry Brigade was disbanded and the 21st Infantry Brigade renumbered as 12th Infantry Brigade.

strength.[36] 6th Armoured Division effectively disappeared in Apr 1958 (although formal disbanding may not have occurred until Jun 1958). Also in Apr 1958, 7th Armoured Division was redesignated 5th Division; concurrently, the 2nd and 4th Divisions dropped "Infantry" from their titles. 10th Infantry Brigade was disbanded and 6th Infantry Brigade shifted again, back to Munster. BAOR then had two armoured brigades (7th and 20th) and five infantry brigades (4th Guards; 5th, 6th, 11th and 12th).

A detailed order of battle for Apr 1958 to Apr 1961 is below at page 51.

Reshuffling of brigades resulted in the following organization ca. Apr 1958:

2nd Division	Hilden
6th Infantry Brigade Group	Munster
11th Infantry Brigade Group	Minden
4th Division	Herford
4th Guards Brigade Group	Hubblerath
5th Infantry Brigade Group	Iserlohn
20th Armoured Brigade Group	Detmold
5th Division	Verden
7th Armoured Brigade Group	Soltau
12th Infantry Brigade Group	Osnabrück

Brigades were restyled in 1958 as brigade groups. The intent was that they would operate more as independent organizations than as sub-formations within divisions. Artillery regiments and engineer squadrons officially moved to the brigades, and the engineer field regiments were disbanded.[37] Each brigade group had a mixed medium/field regiment RA (25-pounders and 5.5" guns). In 1961, each division would gain a mixed regiment with Honest John rockets (two batteries of two launchers each) and towed 8" howitzers (two batteries of four tubes each). Normal division artillery consisted of the towed 25-pounder and 5.5" until the Abbot (105mm SP) began to equip artillery regiments in 1965. A new Army Air Corps was formed 1 Sep 1957. In Germany, each division had a divisional flight and each brigade a reconnaissance flight. These were placed administratively under a squadron designation, although in 1964 the squadrons were redesignated as division aviation.

---

[36] From 77,000 at its peak, BAOR declined to 62,000 and then 56,000 during this period.
[37] This reduced divisions to direct control of a field park squadron RE and their signals, along with supporting units.

In Jun 1960 the 1st Infantry Division was disbanded in England. On 30 Jun 1960 the 5th Division in Germany was redesignated as 1st Division. In Mar 1961 the brigades were reshuffled. The 1st Division was given both of the armoured brigades, gaining 20th Armoured Brigade from 4th Division. In turn, it shifted 12th Infantry Brigade to 2nd Division. Another reshuffling in Mar 1964 sent 20th Armoured Brigade back to 4th Division. Then, in May 1964, headquarters of 5th Infantry Brigade was returned to the UK to help reform a strategic reserve. The next month, 11th Infantry Brigade shifted to 1st Division from the 2nd, remaining at Minden. Headquarters 4th Guards Brigade shifted from Hubblerath to Iserlohn (which had been 5th Infantry Brigade's headquarters location) during 1964.

At this point, the six brigades remaining in BAOR were assigned as follows:

1st Division	Verden
7th Armoured Brigade Group	Soltau
11th Infantry Brigade Group	Minden
2nd Division	Lubbecke
6th Infantry Brigade Group	Munster
12th Infantry Brigade Group	Osnabrück
4th Division	Herford
4th Guards Brigade Group	Iserlohn
20th Armoured Brigade Group	Detmold

According to a Feb 1961 War Office document on the organization of the British Army, the intended organization of various echelons would be:

Infantry Brigade Group: armoured regiment; field artillery regiment; engineer squadron; signal squadron; 3 infantry battalions; recce flight AAC

Armoured Brigade Group: 3 armoured regiments; armoured personnel carrier squadron; medium (SP) artillery regiment; engineer squadron; signal squadron; 1 infantry battalion; recce flight AAC

Division: field park squadron RE; signal regiment; air squadron AAC

Corps: 3 armoured car regiments; 6 armoured personnel carrier squadrons; 4 forward delivery squadrons; ATGW squadron; 2 medium artillery regiments; 1 AGRA (Field) with 2 SSGW regiments, 2 signal squadrons, 1 recce flight; 1 AGRA (AA) with 1 GW regiment, 1 signal sqn, 4 LAA regiments; 1 armoured engineer squadron; 2 corps engineer regiments; corps field park squadron RE; corps signal regiment; corps troops signal regiment; corps signal park; wing HQ AAC with a liaison flight and a recce flight

This does not indicate that BAOR had exactly this organization as of that date, but does show what was intended. A detailed order of battle for the period Apr 1961 to Apr 1964 is below at page 57.

The 4th Canadian Infantry Brigade Group was part of BAOR, originally with 4th Division and shifted 1964 to 2nd Division. It was redesignated as 4th Canadian Mechanised Brigade Group in 1968; in Jun 1971 it relocated to Lahr in southern Germany.[38]

In Nov 1965 the brigade groups were again designated as brigades and clearly brought under divisional control. 6th Infantry Brigade was withdrawn to Barnard Castle in England in Jan 1968 as an economy measure, although remaining assigned to 2nd Division. When it returned to Germany in Mar 1971, it would be as 6th Armoured Brigade. When the 6th left in 1968, 4th Guards Brigade shifted to Munster. Not counting the Canadians, the three divisions had (by Jan 1968) only six brigades, and one of those was in the UK. In Oct 1966 the 7th Armoured and 11th Infantry Brigades engaged in an exercise testing a new brigade organization with two armoured regiments and two mechanised battalions. With the increasing availability of the tracked FV432 APC, all of the infantry battalions in BAOR were to become mechanised.

Components of the divisions and brigades in BAOR were not fixed. Under the British roulement system, units were to change stations at least every six to eight years.[39] Changing station could mean changing organization, from tanks to armoured cars (later armoured recce) for armour, and converting to mechanised for infantry. Armoured regiments and infantry battalions served periodic tours of duty in Germany. For example, 3rd Carabiniers went there in 1952, remaining to 1959; they returned ca. 1961 and remained until 1967. The Royal Scots Greys ended the war in Germany, and stayed until 1952; they returned in 1958 and remained until 1962, and then returned again for the period 1964—1969.[40] Infantry battalions generally averaged somewhat shorter tours, and artillery regiments (especially air defence) generally longer.

---

[38] For details on the Canadian brigade group in Germany, see below at page 63.

[39] At least in the 1970s there was an intended 14-year scheme for infantry battalions: Years 1-4 BAOR; Years 5-6 UK home defence; Years 7-8 Northern Ireland; Years 9-10 overseas garrison; Years 11-14 UK- ACE, UKMF, BAOR reinforcement. To what extent this was actually followed for any battalion is unclear. While typically rotations were to or from BAOR, units could be shifted around while in Germany, between formations or even between locations. At this date it has proven very difficult to pin down the location and assignments of all units in Germany for the period before the 1970s, and there are questions and gaps even for more recent periods.

[40] Units of the RTR could serve very long tours in Germany, especially when they were restricted to equipment as tank units (the armoured car role was restricted to cavalry

However, even units in BAOR could be pulled for other duties as needed. Thus 1st Bn Coldstream Guards, assigned BOAR but in Libya for an exercise in 1965, was pulled for a six-month tour in Aden before returning to Germany. The continuing troubles in Northern Ireland from 1969 resulted in a number of units being pulled for short-term security duties in that province.[41] Since BAOR had the only infantry mounted in the FV432, battalions transferring to Germany had to reorganize as mechanised and then learn to make use of (and service) the APCs and other vehicles.

There were gradual changes after 1965. The 1966 experiment with a new organization has already been noted. By the end of 1970 the six brigades in BAOR had been redesignated as 4th, 6th, 7th, 11th and 20th Armoured and 12th Mechanised, still grouped under the 1st, 2nd and 4th Divisions.[42] Armoured brigades had two armoured regiments and two mechanised infantry battalions. The mechanised brigade had one armoured regiment and three mechanised infantry battalions. Brigades had a command element and a small aviation unit (with six-nine light helicopters). Artillery and engineers were grouped under division control. In 1969, engineers were reorganized into two regiments (of two field squadrons each) with the field park squadron retained under division RE. This had the effect of doubling the engineer support for each brigade. Another change, in Oct 1969, resulted in division aviation becoming regiments AAC (bearing the division number). Each new regiment had three squadrons AAC. The squadrons absorbed former brigade and division flights, along with air troops from various divisional units. Thus, the overall number of aircraft may not have changed significantly, but all were now grouped in a single unit under division control.

A detailed order of battle for the period Apr 1964 to Dec 1970 begins below at page 65.

---

regiments until the early 1960s). Thus, for example, 3rd RTR was in BAOR from Oct 1952 to Aug 1962 and 4th RTR there from Sep 1954 to Dec 1962.
[41] Almost any type of unit (infantry, armour, artillery, engineers, transport) could find itself tasked for a tour as infantry in Northern Ireland. As the Army was reduced and other demands grew, the process of conversion and auxiliary tasks only grew worse. For example, 3rd Bn The Light Infantry was sent to Minden in Feb 1990 to equip with the new Warrior MCV. This was interrupted with the need to train reinforcements for the Gulf War that autumn. With no Warriors available, their tour in Northern Ireland was moved up to May 1991. In Nov 1991 they returned to Germany, where there were still insufficient Warrior vehicles. Not until Aug 1992 did the battalion begin training on the Warrior [now termed an ICV]. Thus, BAOR was short one armoured infantry battalion for nearly two and a half years.
[42] 4th Armoured Brigade may have been 4th Guards Armoured Brigade for a period, or simply referred to as such, but "Guards" did disappear from its title. 6th Brigade probably did not redesignate until it returned to Germany Mar 1971.

Support

There were some separate artillery regiments in Germany from the beginning, medium regiments and the single locating regiment. There was no distinct headquarters [army group RA] for field artillery units in BAOR. Medium regiments had the wartime towed 5.5" guns. 42nd Medium Regiment RA came to Germany Oct 1962 still with the 5.5" guns but then converted Mar 1969 to the M109 (SP 155mm howitzers). 32nd Heavy Regiment RA had come to Germany in Apr 1966 with the M107 (SP 175mm Guns) and would be joined in Jan 1968 by another regiment with the M107.

HQ 1st AGRA (Field) deployed to Germany 1961, with headquarters at Hildesheim. The headquarters was redesignated 4 Oct 1961 as 1st Artillery Brigade (Field), and by Jan 1967 it was simply 1st Artillery Brigade. It was initially responsible for the two Corporal SSM regiments, along with a support regiment. (From 1959, BAOR had two regiments with Corporal missiles.) It gradually evolved from a command unit solely for the Corporal missile regiments to one for all GHQ field artillery in 1 Corps. The Corporal-equipped regiments were in addition to the three mixed regiments with Honest John rockets and 8" howitzers found in the divisions.

GHQ air defence units initially came under command of 5th Army Group RA (AA), which was formed 1 Nov 1950 in BAOR by redesignation of 5th AA Brigade. At its peak it had three heavy AA and two light AA regiments, and was still at that strength in 1955. 5th Army Group RA (AA) was inactivated 31 Mar 1958, along with the general reduction in AA units throughout the British Army.

In Sep 1961 7th Army Group RA (AA) moved to Germany. That unit was redesignated 4 Oct 1961 as 7th Artillery Brigade (AA); headquarters was at Gütersloh. 36th Heavy AA Regiment RA was converted 1 Apr 1959 in the UK to 36th Guided Weapons Regiment (AA) RA and 37th Heavy AA Regiment RA was converted 1 Oct 1959 to 37th Guided Weapons Regiment (AA) RA. Both were equipped with the Thunderbird SAM; the 36th went to Germany and later returned to the UK. On 18 Mar 1964 their designations were changed to Heavy Air Defense Regiments RA and on 1 Apr 1968 they were consolidated into a single regiment, the 36th, which had another tour in Germany before being disbanded. Light air defense (formerly light AA) regiments were equipped with 40mm Bofors guns.[43]

---

[43] In 1961 all RA regiments dropped type designators such as "field" or "light AA" from their designations. When these designations reappeared in Mar 1964, anti-aircraft (AA) had become air defence (AD).

As noted earlier, the theoretical organization for artillery (excluding anything that might have been directly subordinated to BAOR itself) was two medium artillery regiments; one AGRA (Field) with two SSGW regiments; and one AGRA (AA) with one GW regiment and four LAA regiments.

The Army Air Corps was created in 1957 from Air Observation Post (AOP) squadrons of the RAF and The Glider Pilot Regiment (whose members had been flying light aircraft alongside the RAF).[44] The bulk of the units in Germany ended up under division control, designated in turn as squadrons, division aviation, and then regiments. There was a wing headquarters established at BAOR, which later became HQ Army Aviation, BAOR. Actual GHQ units comprised two flights, one serving as BAOR HQ Flight.

Supporting RE organization was fairly stable until 1969, with 11 Engineer Group and two regiments, along with some support units under 40 Engineer Stores Regiment. At the beginning of the period there had been some effort to rotate the non-divisional regiments between BAOR and elsewhere, but this was abandoned in 1959 as disruptive and impractical. A specialized regiment to control armoured engineer units was formed in 1964, the same year an amphibious engineer squadron moved to BAOR. In 1969, the armoured engineer regiment and the two corps engineer regiments were both reorganized as part of divisional RE, virtually eliminating any GHQ engineer elements.

While the number and roles of signals regiments was fairly stable, the units themselves went through a number of designation changes. At the beginning of the period, designations were either based on the formation served or on separate numbering systems based on the unit's role. In Sep 1959, all of the regiments in the Royal Corps of Signals were placed in a single numbering system; Regular regiments and had numbers between 1 and 30, and squadrons not part of a regiment were numbered from 200 upwards. In 1965, the Royal Signals took over responsibility for division and brigade headquarters. Thus, from two separate units you then had designations such as "1st Armoured Division Headquarters and Signal Regiment" or "7th Armoured Brigade Headquarters and 207th Signal Squadron."[45]

---

[44] In fact, The Glider Pilot Regiment actually provided most of the pilots, and the RAF's major connection to these units was maintenance tasks. Only No. 652 Squadron remained active in Germany after the war. The Army Air Corps took over the old AOP squadron numbers (651-666) from the RAF.

[45] An alternative form, when squadrons had numbers, would be to show it as "7th Armoured Brigade Headquarters and Signal Squadron (207)."

In the service role, the Royal Army Service Corps (RASC)—in charge of most supply and transport units—was merged in 1965 with some transport elements of the Royal Engineers to form the new Royal Corps of Transport (RCT).

Formation Signs, BAOR at its Peak

1 Corps

2nd Infantry Division

6th Armoured Division

7th Armoured Division

11th Armoured Division

Rhine Army Troops

BAOR 1951—Mar 1956

HQ BAOR   *Bad Oyenhausen*; Oct 1954 to *Rheindahlen*
HQ BAOR Signal Regt   *Bad Oyenhausen*
      redesignated Apr 1952 as HQ NORTHAG Signal Regt
      redesignated 1953 as 18th Army Group Signal Regt
4th LoC Signal Regt [formed 1952]   *Herford*
      redesignated 1953 as 19th Army Group Signal Regt
11th Air Formation Signal Regt   *Lemgo*
83 Group Signal Regt   *Wahn*
      redesignated 1953 as 12th Air Formation Signal Regt
1st Wireless Regt   *Munster*; May 1955 to *Birgelen*
2nd LoC Signal Regt   *Düsseldorf*

40 Advanced Engr Stores Regt [formed 1952]   *Wilich*
      80, 1254, 1255 Wksp Sqns and 339 Plant Sqn RE
14 Field Survey Sqn RE   *Mönchen-Gladbach*

HQ 1 Corps [formed Nov 1951]   *Bielefeld*
1 Corps Signal Regt   *Bad Oyenhausen*

1st King's Dragoon Guards [recce]   *Hamburg* [left Jun 1952]
15/19th Hussars [recce]   *Lubbecke*; Apr 1951 to *Hamburg* and Nov
      1951 to *Neumuster* [left Jun 1954 w/o replacement]
1st King's Dragoon Gds [recce] [arrived Jan 1955]   *Neumunster* [left Mar
      1956]

15th Medium Regt RA   *Lippstadt*
      7, 38 Mdm Btys RA [5.5"]
      replaced Mar 1955 by 58th Medium Regt RA {118, 175 Mdm
          Btys RA}
24th Medium Regt RA [arrived Jan 1956]   *Nienburg*
      2, 51, 128 Mdm Btys RA [5.5"]
94th Loc Regt RA   *Munsterlager*; 1955 to *Hildesheim*
      210, 211 Loc Btys RA[46]

---

[46] Regiment reduced May 1955 to 112 Loc Bty.

⌒ **5th AGRA (AA)** [arrived Feb 1951]   *Delmenhorst*
77th HAA Regt RA [arrived Feb 1951]   *Delmenhorst*
          209, 221, 222 HAA Btys RA[47]
44th HAA Regt RA [arrived Sep 1951]   *Oldenburg*
          46, 153, 154 HAA Btys RA
30th HAA Regt RA [arrived 1952]   *Delmenhorst*
          76, 77, 85 HAA Btys RA
35th LAA Regt RA [arrived 1952]   *Oldenburg*; Apr 1955 to *Adelheide*
          90, 92, 99 LAA Btys RA [40mm]
74th LAA Regt RA [arrived 1952]   *Aurich*; Apr 1955 to *Adelheide*
          200, 202, 230, 231 LAA Btys RA [40mm]
72nd LAA Regt RA [arrived Jul 1955]   *Oldenburg*
          6, 42, 44, 91 LAA Btys RA [40mm]

⊡ **11 Engineer Group** [formed 1951]*Osnabrück*
37 Army Engr Regt [arrived 1951]   *Osnabrück* [left 1955]
          33, 34, 40 Field Sqns and 41 Field Pk Sqn RE
38 Corps Engr Regt [arrived 1951]   *Osnabrück*
          61, 62, 63 Field Sqns RE
65 Corps Field Park Sqn RE [from 1953]   *Osnabrück*

⊠ **2nd Infantry Division**
HQ 2nd Infantry Division   *Hilden*
2nd Infantry Division Signal Regt   *Hilden*
10th Hussars [recce]   *Iserlohn*
          replaced Jul 1953 by 3rd Hussars
19th Field Regt RA   *Düsseldorf*
          25, 28, 67 Field Btys RA [25pdr]
          replaced Sep 1954 by 29th Field Regt RA {8, 79, 145 Field Btys RA}
40th Field Regt RA   *Dortmund*
          78, 109, 129 Field Btys RA [25pdr]
          replaced Dec 1954 by 45th Field Regt RA {70, 116, 176 Fd Btys RA}
42nd Field Regt RA   *Essen*
          68, 87, 159 Field Btys RA [25pdr]
          replaced Nov 1953 by 48th Field Regt RA {75, 95, 201 Fd Btys RA}
          replaced Sep 1955 by 41st Field Regt RA {85, 105, 165 Fd Btys RA}

---

[47] 209 and 222 Btys became 29 and 41 Btys in Apr 1955 and 37 HAA Bty RA joined in Jun 1955.

[2nd Infantry Division]
22nd LAA Regt RA   *Menden*
      47, 48, 53 LAA Btys RA [40mm]
115th Loc Bty RA   *Dortmund*
'Z' Lt Mortar Bty RA   *Menden*; 1953 to *Dortmund*
23 Field Engr Regt: *Dortmund*
      2, 5, 38 Field Sqns and 21 Field Park Sqn RE

HQ 4th GUARDS BRIGADE   *Hubblerath*
2nd Bn Grenadier Gds   *Krefeld*
      replaced Nov 1952 by 2nd Bn Coldstream Gds
      replaced Mar 1955 by 1st Bn Coldstream Gds
1st Bn Royal Norfolk Regt   *Hubblerath*
      replaced Feb 1951 by 1st Bn Irish Gds
      replaced Feb 1954 by 1st Bn East Lancashire Regt
      replaced Mar 1955 by 1st Bn Grenadier Gds
1st Bn Welsh Gds   *Hubblerath*
      replaced Mar 1952 by 2nd Bn Black Watch
      replaced Jul 1953 by 2nd Bn Scots Gds

HQ 5th INFANTRY BRIGADE   *Iserlohn*
1st Bn Queen's Royal Regt   *Iserlohn*
      replaced 1953 by 1st Bn Lancashire Fusiliers
1st Bn Royal Fusiliers   *Iserlohn* [left Jun 1952]
      replaced Oct 1952 by 1st Bn Royal Leicestershire Regt
      replaced Jan 1955 by 1st Bn Worcestershire Regt
1st Bn Durham LI   *Dortmund*
      replaced Sep 1951 by 1st Bn KO Yorkshire LI
      replaced Jul 1953 by 2nd Bn Black Watch
      replaced Sep 1954 by 1st Bn Royal Welch Fusiliers

HQ 6th INFANTRY BRIGADE   *Munster*; Dec 1951 to *Wuppertal*
1st Bn Black Watch   *Duisburg*
      replaced Feb 1951 by 1st Bn Royal Scots at *Munster*; Dec 1951
          to *Wuppertal*
      replaced May 1952 by 2nd Bn Sherwood Foresters
      replaced May 1954 by 1st Bn Suffolk Regt
1st Bn Worcestershire Regt   *Wuppertal*
      replaced Jan 1951 by 1st Bn Somerset LI
      replaced Jan 1953 by 1st Bn Northamptonshire Regt
      replaced Jun 1955 by 1st Bn Royal Ulster Rifles

[6th Infantry Brigade]
1st Bn Royal Scots Fusiliers   *Munster*; 1952 to *Wuppertal*
        replaced Jul 1953 by 2nd Bn Durham LI
        replaced Mar 1955 by 1st Bn Buffs

6th Armoured Division[48]

HQ 6th Armoured Division   *Herford*, 1953 to *Bunde*
6th Armoured Division Signal Regt   *Bunde*
1st King's Dragoon Gds [recce] [joined Jun 1952]   *Neumunster*
        replaced Jan 1955 by 12th Lancers at *Herford*; to *Neumunster* Mar 1956
3rd Carabiniers [atk regt]   *Osnabrück*
5th Field Regt RHA [arrived May 1951] *Osnabrück*
        C, G, K Btys RHA [Sexton]
1st Field Regt RHA   [arrived May 1952] *Munster*
        A, B, E Btys RHA [Sexton]
16th LAA Regt RA   *Osnabrück* [left Mar 1956]
        26, 30, 32 LAA Btys RA [40mm]
156th Loc Bty RA   *Osnabrück*
27 Field Engr Regt   *Minden*
        1, 25, 28 Field Sqns and 44 Field Park Sqn RE

HQ 20th ARMOURED BRIGADE   *Munster*
17th/21st Lancers [arrived Sep 1951]   *Munster*
2nd Royal Tank Regt [arrived Feb 1952] *Munster*
6th Royal Tank Regt [arrived Jan 1952]   *Munster*
        replaced Feb 1956 by 14th/20th Hussars
2nd Bn KRRC [arrived Feb 1952]   *Munster*

HQ 61st LORRIED INFANTRY BRIGADE   *Minden*
1st Bn KORR   *Osnabrück*
        replaced Sep 1953 by 1st Bn Oxford and Bucks LI
        replaced Mar 1956 by 1st Bn Duke of Cornwall's LI
1st Bn Duke of Cornwall's LI   *Minden*
        replaced Oct 1953 by 1st Bn Green Howards
        replaced Feb 1956 by 1st Bn Manchester Regt

---

[48] The division moved to Germany and BAOR in early 1952. Division HQ opened at Herford in Feb 1952 and other elements arrived about the same time unless shown differently. The division had been formed the year before.

[61st Lorried Infantry Brigade]
1st Bn Duke of Wellington's Regt [arrived Dec 1951]   *Minden*
      replaced Oct 1952 by 1st Bn South Staffordshire Regt
      replaced Jun 1954 by 1st Bn Royal Sussex Regt
      replaced Mar 1956 by 1st Bn Dorset Regt

⬚ **7th Armoured Division**
HQ 7th Armoured Division   *Verden*
7th Armoured Division Signal Regt   *Verden*
11th Hussars [recce]   *Wesendorf* [left Jul 1953]
      replaced Mar 1953 by 15th/19th Hussars
      replaced Apr 1954 by The Royal Dragoons at *Warendorf*
7th Hussars [atk regt]   *Luneburg*; Oct 1951 to *Fallingbostel*
      replaced Jun 1954 by 4th/7th Dragoon Gds
3rd Field Regt RHA   *Munsterlager*
      D, J, M Btys RHA [Sexton]
      replaced Apr 1954 by 6th Field Regt RA at *Hohne* {H, V, W Field
           Btys RA}
4th Field Regt RHA   *Hohne*
      F, N, P Btys RHA [Sexton]
12th LAA Regt RA   *Celle* [to corps troops Mar 1956]
      T, 9, 34 LAA Btys RA [40mm]
204th Loc Bty RA   *Munsterlager*
21 Field Engr Regt   *Nienburg*
      4, 27, 48 Field Sqns and 45 Field Park Sqn RE

HQ 7th ARMOURED BRIGADE   *Soltau*
Queen's Bays   *Fallingbostel*
      replaced Jul 1954 by 4th Royal Tank Regt
 Royal Scots Greys   *Luneburg*
      replaced Apr 1952 by 8th Hussars
      replaced Mar 1956 by 4th/7th Dragoon Guards
5th Royal Tank Regt   *Hohne*
      replaced Sep 1953 by 4th Hussars
1st Bn Rifle Brigade   *Celle*
      replaced Oct 1953 by 2nd Bn Sherwood Foresters
      replaced Jun 1955 by 1st Bn Devonshire Regt

HQ 31st L<small>ORRIED</small> I<small>NFANTRY</small> B<small>RIGADE</small>   *Minden*; Oct 1951 to *Luneburg*
1st Bn East Yorkshire Regt   *Buxtehude* [left Dec 1951]
       replaced Feb 1952 by 1st Bn Black Watch
       replaced Apr 1952 by 1st Bn Seaforth Highlanders
       replaced Jul 1954 by 1st Bn Cameronians
1st Bn Royal Hampshire Regt   *Minden*; Oct 1951 to *Luneburg*
       replaced Aug 1953 by 1st Bn QO Cameron Highlanders
       replaced Jul 1955 by 1st Bn East Lancashire Regt
1st Bn Essex Regt [arrived Apr 1951]   *Minden*; Oct 1951 to *Luneburg*
       replaced Aug 1953 by 2nd Bn Royal Welch Fusiliers
       replaced Aug 1954 by 1st Bn QOR West Kent Regt

⊡ 11th **Armoured Division**

HQ 11th Armoured Division   *Herford*
11th Armoured Division Signal Regt   *Herford*
Royal Horse Guards [recce]   *Wolfenbüttel*
       replaced Mar 1952 by Life Guards
       replaced Jul 1953 by 13th/18th Hussars [left Mar 1956]
3rd Hussars [atk regt]   *Bielefeld*
       replaced Jul 1953 by 16th/5th Lancers at *Sennelager*
2nd Field Regt RHA   *Hildesheim*
       I, L, O Btys RHA [Sexton]
10th Field Regt RA   *Detmold*
       Q, X, Y Btys RA [Sexton]
53rd LAA Regt RA   *Lippstadt*
       58, 106, 110 LAA Btys RA [40mm]
157th Loc Bty RA   *Hildesheim*
26 Field Engr Regt RE   *Hameln*
       7, 29, 60 Field Sqns and 43 Field Park Sqn RE

HQ 33rd A<small>RMOURED</small> B<small>RIGADE</small>   *Bad Lippspringe*
5th Royal Inniskilling Dragoon Gds   *Paderborn*
       replaced Aug 1951 by 8th Royal Tank Regt
1st Royal Tank Regt   *Detmold*
       replaced Oct 1952 by 3rd Royal Tank Regt
9th Lancers [assigned Nov 1952]   *Detmold*
1st Bn KRRC   *Sennelager*
       replaced Jun 1955 by 1st Bn Sherwood Foresters at *Bad Lippspringe*

HQ 91st LORRIED INFANTRY BRIGADE   *Hildesheim*
1st Bn Sherwood Foresters   *Goslar*
        replaced 1953 by 1st Bn Royal Lincolnshire Regt
        replaced Jun 1954 by 1st Bn Royal Berkshire Regt
1st Bn York & Lancaster Regt   *Brunswick*
        replaced Jan 1953 by 1st Bn South Wales Borderers
        replaced Jul 1955 by 1st Bn East Surrey Regt
1st Bn Royal Irish Fusiliers   *Gottingen*
        replaced Oct 1952 by 1st Bn King's Shropshire LI
        replaced Mar 1955 by 1st Bn Border Regt

Note: From Dec 1951 there was also a Canadian infantry brigade group assigned to BAOR. The Canadian force is discussed below on page 63.

▭ *BAOR Apr 1956—Sep 1957*

HQ BAOR   *Rheindahlen*
14th Army Signal Regt [formed 1955, disbanded 1957]   *Lemgo*
18th Army Group Signal Regt   *Bad Oyenhausen*
19th Army Group Signal Regt   *Herford*
10th Air Formation Signal Regt   *Melsbroeck*
11th Air Formation Signal Regt   *Lemgo*
12th Air Formation Signal Regt   *Laarbuch*
1st Wireless Regt   *Birgelen*
2nd Line of Communications Signal Regt   *Düsseldorf*

40 Advanced Engr Stores Regt   *Wilich*
        80, 1254, 1255 Wksp Sqns and 339 Plant Sqn RE
14 Field Survey Sqn RE   *Mönchen-Gladbach*

HQ 1 Corps   *Bielefeld*
1 Corps Signal Regt   *Bad Oyenhausen*

13th/18th Hussars [recce, AFNORTH]   *Lubbecke*

24th Medium Regt RA[49]   *Luneburg*; Aug 1957 to *Nienburg*
        2, 51, 56 Mdm Btys RA [5.5"]
58th Medium Regt RA[50]   *Menden*
        118, 175 Mdm Btys RA[51] [5.5"]
94th Locating Regt RA   *Celle*
        112 Loc Bty RA
12th LAA Regt RA   *Celle*; Nov 1956 to *Hereford*
        T, 9, 34 LAA Btys RA [40mm]

⌂ **5th AGRA (AA)**   *Delmenhorst*
30th HAA Regt RA   *Delmenhorst*
        76, 77, 85 HAA Btys RA
44th HAA Regt RA   *Oldenburg*
        116, 153, 154 HAA Btys RA
77th HAA Regt RA   *Delmenhorst*
        29, 37, 41, 221 HAA Btys RA[52]

---

[49] Under operational control of 4th Infantry Division.
[50] Under operational control of 2nd Infantry Division to May 1957.
[51] Added Z Mdm Bty RA Apr 1956.
[52] 221 HAA Bty RA disbanded 1 Jul 1957.

[5th AGRA (AA)]
35th LAA Regt RA   *Adelheide*
        90, 92, 99 LAA Btys RA [40mm]
72nd LAA Regt RA   *Adelheide*
        6, 42, 44, 91 LAA Btys RA [40mm]
150th AA Fire Control Bty RA   *location unknown*
19th AA C&A Trp RA   *location unknown*

11 Engineer Group   *Osnabrück*
36 Corps Engr Regt   *Osnabrück*
        20, 24, 57 Field Sqns RE
38 Corps Engr Regt   *Osnabrück*
        61, 62, 63 Field Sqns RE
35 Corps Engr Regt [arrived 1957]   *Osnabrück*
        16, 30, 42 Field Sqns RE
26 Assault Sqn RE   [arrived ca. Jul 1957?]   *Hohne?*
41 Army Field Pk Sqn RE   *Osnabrück*
65 Corps Field Pk Sqn RE   *Osnabrück*

2nd Infantry Division
HQ 2nd Infantry Division   *Hilden*
2nd Infantry Division Signal Regt   *Hilden*
29th Field Regt RA   *Düsseldorf* <for CS 4th Brigade>
        8, 79, 145 Field Btys RA [25pdr]
        replaced May 1957 by 40th Field Regt RA{78, 109, 129 Fd Btys RA}
41st Field Regt RA   *Essen* <for CS 6th Brigade>
        88, 105, 165 Field Btys RA [25pdr]
45th Field Regt RA   *Dortmund* <for CS 5th Brigade>
        70, 116, 176 Field Btys RA [25pdr]
12th LAA Regt RA   *Dortmund*
        T, 9, 34 LAA Btys RA [40mm]
115th Loc Bty RA   *location unknown*
23 Field Engr Regt RE   *Lubbecke*
        2, 5, 38 Field Sqns and 21 Field Park Sqn RE

HQ 4th G<small>UARDS</small> B<small>RIGADE</small>   *Hubblerath*
16th/5th Lancers   *Sennelager*
     replaced Mar 1957 by 5th R Inniskilling Dragoon Gds
     replaced Aug 1957 by 17th/21st Lancers
1st Bn Grenadier Gds   *Hubblerath*
     replaced Jan 1957 by 1st Bn KO Yorkshire LI
1st Bn Coldstream Gds   *Hubblerath*
2nd Bn Scots Guards   *Hubblerath*
     replaced Jan 1957 by 3rd Bn Coldstream Guards

HQ 5th I<small>NFANTRY</small> B<small>RIGADE</small>   *Iserlohn*
3rd Hussars   *Iserlohn*; Sep 1957 to *Munster*
1st Bn Lancashire Fusiliers   *Iserlohn*
     replaced Jan 1957 by 1st Bn Royal Norfolk Regt
1st Bn Royal Welch Fusiliers   *Dortmund*
     replaced Aug 1956 by 1st Bn Essex Regt
1st Bn Worcestershire Regt   *Iserlohn*
     replaced Feb 1957 by 1st Bn Queens Royal Regt at *Minden*

HQ 6th I<small>NFANTRY</small> B<small>RIGADE</small>   *Munster*
8th Royal Tank Regt   *Paderborn*
     replaced Feb 1957 by 2nd Royal Tank Regt
1st Bn The Buffs   *Wuppertal*
1st Bn Suffolk Regt   *Wuppertal*
     replaced Jul 1956 by 1st Bn R Scots Fusiliers [left Aug 1957]
1st Bn Royal Ulster Rifles   *Wuppertal*
     replaced Jun 1956 by 1st Bn Royal Irish Fusiliers

⊠ 4th Infantry Division

HQ 4th Infantry Division   *Herford*
4th Infantry Division Signal Regt   *Herford*
2nd Field Regt RHA   *Hildesheim* <for CS 12th Brigade>
     I, L, O Btys RHA [25pdr]
6th Field Regt RA   *Munsterlager* <for CS 10th Brigade>
     H, V, W Field Btys RA [25pdr]
10th Field Regt RA   *Detmold* <for CS 11th Brigade>
     Q, X, Y Field Btys RA [25pdr]
53rd LAA Regt RA   *Lippstadt*
     56, 106, 110 LAA Btys RA [40mm]
157th Loc Bty RA   *location unknown*

[4th Infantry Division]
26 Field Engr Regt RE   *Paderborn*
      7, 29, 60 Field Sqns and 43 Field Park Sqn RE

HQ 10th INFANTRY BRIGADE   *Hildesheim*
8th Hussars   *Lüneburg*
1st Bn Cameronians   *Luneburg*
1st Bn QO Royal West Kent Regt   *Minden*
      replaced Jun 1956 by 1st Bn Welch Regt
1st Bn East Lancashire Regt   *Luneburg*
      replaced Apr 1957 by 1st Bn Highland LI

HQ 11TH INFANTRY BRIGADE   *Minden*
9th Lancers   *Detmold*
1st Bn Sherwood Foresters   *Bad Lippspringe*
1st Bn Dorset Regt [arrived Apr 1956]   *Minden*
1st Bn Manchester Regt   *Minden*

HQ 12th INFANTRY BRIGADE   *Osnabrück*
3rd Royal Tank Regt   *Detmold*
1st Bn Border Regt   *Gottingen*
1st Bn East Surrey Regt   *Brunswick*
1st Bn R Berkshire Regt   *Goslar*
      replaced May 1956 by 1st Bn Bedfords & Herts Regt

6th Armoured Division

HQ 6th Armoured Division   *Bunde*
6th Armoured Division Signal Regt   *Bunde*
12th Lancers [recce]   *Neumunster*
3rd Carabiniers   *Osnabrück*
14th/20th Hussars   *Munster*
17th/21st Lancers   *Munster*
2nd Royal Tank Regt   *Munster*
2nd Bn KRRC   *Munster*
      replaced Aug 1956 by 1st Bn R Hampshire Regt
1st Field Regt RHA   *Munster*
      A, B, E Btys RHA [M44]
27 Field Engr Regt RE   *Minden*
      1, 25 and 28 Field Sqns RE and 44 Field Park Sqn RE

⬚ 7ᵗʰ Armoured Division

HQ 7ᵗʰ Armoured Division   *Verden*
7ᵗʰ Armoured Division Signal Regt   *Verden*
The Royal Dragoons [recce]   *Warendorf*
4ᵗʰ/7ᵗʰ Dragoon Gds   *Fallingbostel*
4ᵗʰ Hussars   *Hohne*
4ᵗʰ Royal Tank Regt   *Fallingbostel*
13ᵗʰ/18ᵗʰ Hussars [recce]   *location unknown*
17ᵗʰ/21ˢᵗ Lancers   *Fallingbostel*
1ˢᵗ Bn Devonshire Regt   *Celle*
4ᵗʰ Field Regt RHA   *Hohne*
    F, N, P Btys RHA [M44]
21 Field Engr Regt RE   *Nienburg*
    4, 27, and 48 Field Sqns and 45 Field Park Sqn RE

⊠ 21ˢᵗ Independent Infantry Brigade[53]   *Osnabrück*

1ˢᵗ Bn King's Regt   *Osnabrück*]
1ˢᵗ Bn East Yorkshire Regt   *Osnabrück*
1ˢᵗ Bn Oxford and Bucks LI   *Osnabrück*
5ᵗʰ Field Regt RHA   *Osnabrück*
    C, G, K Btys RHA [Sexton]

---

[53] This brigade was formed ca. Mar 1956 in Germany [some sources have shown it formed as late as Apr 1957].

⬜ *BAOR Sep 1957—Apr 1958*

HQ BAOR   *Rheindahlen*
18th Army Group Signal Regt   *Bad Oyenhausen*
19th Army Group Signal Regt   *Herford*
10th Air Formation Signal Regt   *Melsbroeck*
11th Air Formation Signal Regt   *Lemgo*
12th Air Formation Signal Regt   *Laarbuch*
1st Wireless Regt   *Birgelen*
2nd Line of Communications Signal Regt   *Düsseldorf*

40 Advanced Engr Stores Regt   *Wilich*
      80, 1254, 1255 Wksp Sqns and 339 Plant Sqn RE
14 Field Survey Sqn RE   *Mönchen-Gladbach*

13th/18th Hussars [recce, AFNORTH]   *Lubbecke*

HQ 1 Corps   *Bielefeld*
1 Corps Signal Regt   *Bad Oyenhausen*

The Royal Dragoons [recce]   *Warendorf*
12th Lancers [recce]   *Neumunster*
14th/20th Hussars [APC regt Sep 1957[54]]   *Munster*

24th Medium Regt RA   *Nienburg*
      2, 51, 128 Mdm Btys RA [5.5"]
58th Medium Regt RA   *Menden*
      Z, 118, 175 Mdm Btys RA[55] [5.5"]
94th Locating Regt RA   *Celle*
      112 Loc Bty RA
12th LAA Regt RA   *Herford*; moved Oct 1957 to *Lippstadt*
      T, 9, 34 LAA Btys RA [40mm]

---

[54] Only RHQ at Munster; APC squadrons ('A' and 'C')at Lemgo and Celle and tank squadron ('B') in Berlin.
[55] Added L Medium Bty RA Nov 1957.

⬚ **5ᵗʰ AGRA (AA)** [disbanded Mar 1958]   *Delmenhorst*
30ᵗʰ HAA Regt RA [disbanded Jan 1958]   *Delmenhorst*
       76, 77, 85 HAA Btys RA
44ᵗʰ HAA Regt RA [disbanded Jan 1958]   *Delmenhorst*
       116, 153, 154 HAA Btys RA
77ᵗʰ HAA Regt RA [disbanded Jan 1958]   *Delmenhorst*
       29, 37, 41, 221 HAA Btys RA
35ᵗʰ LAA Regt RA   *Oldenburg*
       90, 92, 99 LAA Btys RA [40mm]
72ⁿᵈ LAA Regt RA [disbanded Mar 1958]   *Adelheide*
       6, 42, 44, 91 LAA Btys RA [40mm]
150ᵗʰ AA Fire Control Bty RA   *location unknown*

🔲 **11 Engineer Group**   *Osnabrück*
35 Corps Engr Regt   *Osnabrück*
      16, 30, 42 Field Sqns RE
36 Corps Engr Regt   *Osnabrück*
      20, 24, 57 Field Sqns RE
38 Corps Engr Regt   *Osnabrück*
      61, 62, 63 Field Sqns RE
26 Assault Sqn RE   *Hohne?*
65 Corps Field Pk Sqn RE   *Osnabrück*

⊠ **2ⁿᵈ Infantry Division**
HQ 2ⁿᵈ Infantry Division   *Hilden*
2ⁿᵈ Infantry Division Signal Regt   *Hilden*
23 Field Engr Regt RE   *Lubbecke*
      2, 5, 38 Field Sqns and 21 Field Park Sqn RE

HQ 4ᵗʰ GUARDS BRIGADE   *Hubblerath*
17ᵗʰ/21ˢᵗ Lancers   *Munster*
1ˢᵗ Bn Coldstream Gds   *Hubblerath*
3ʳᵈ Bn Coldstream Guards   *Hubblerath*
1ˢᵗ Bn KO Yorkshire LI *Hubblerath*
40ᵗʰ Field Regt RA   *Dortmund*
      78, 109, 129 Field Btys RA [25pdr]
29 Field Sqn RE from 26 Field Engr Regt of 4ᵗʰ Infantry Division

HQ 5th INFANTRY BRIGADE   *Iserlohn*
3rd Hussars   *Munster*
1st Bn Queens Royal Regt   *Iserlohn*
1st Bn Royal Norfolk Regt   *Iserlohn*
1st Bn Essex Regt   *Dortmund*
45th Field Regt RA   *Dortmund*
       70, 116, 176 Field Btys RA [25pdr]
5 Field Sqn RE from 23 Field Engr Regt of 2nd Infantry Division

HQ 6th INFANTRY BRIGADE[56]   *Wuppertal*
8th Royal Tank Regt   *Paderborn*
      replaced Sep 1957 by 2nd Royal Tank Regt at *Munster*
1st Bn R Northumberland Fusiliers   *Wuppertal*
1st Bn Seaforth Highlanders   *Wuppertal*
1st Bn Royal Irish Fusiliers   *Wuppertal*
41st Field Regt RA   *Essen*
      88, 105, 165 Field Btys RA [25pdr]
2 Field Sqn RE from 23 Field Engr Regt of 2nd Infantry Division

⊠ 4th Infantry Division

HQ 4th Infantry Division   *Herford*
4th Infantry Division Signal Regt   *Herford*
53rd LAA Regt RA   *Lippstadt* [left Dec 1957]
      56, 106, 110 LAA Btys RA [40mm]
26 Field Engr Regt RE   *Paderborn*
      7, 29, 60 Field Sqns and 43 Field Park Sqn RE

HQ 11TH INFANTRY BRIGADE   *Minden*
7th Royal Tank Regt   *Detmold*
1st Bn Dorset Regt   *Minden*
1st Bn Sherwood Foresters   *Bad Lippspringe*
1st Bn Manchester Regt   *Minden*
      replaced Sep 1957 by 1st Bn North Staffordshire Regt
10th Field Regt RA   *Detmold*
      Q, X, Y Field Btys RA [25pdr]
      replaced Dec 1957 by 19th Field Regt RA at *Minden* {25, 28, 67 Fd
          Btys RA}
25 Field Sqn RE from 27 Field Engr Regt of 6th Armoured Division

---

[56] 1st Bn The Buffs and 1st Bn Suffolk Regt both left Aug-Sep 1957 and were replaced
by 1st Bn R Northumberland Fusiliers and 1st Bn Seaforth Highlanders.

HQ 12th INFANTRY BRIGADE[57]   *Hildesheim*
3rd Carabiniers   *Osnabrück* [to new 12th Brigade}
1st Bn Bedfords and Hertfords Regt   *Goslar* [left Nov 1957]
[12th Infantry Brigade]
1st Bn Border Regt   *Gottingen*
1st Bn East Surrey Regt   *Brunswick*
2nd Field Regt RHA[58]   *Hildesheim*
       I, L, O Btys RHA [25pdr]

HQ 21st [12th] INFANTRY BRIGADE[59]   *Osnabrück*
3rd Carabiniers [assigned Jan 1958]   *Osnabrück*
1st Bn King's Regt   *Osnabrück* [left Feb 1958]
1st Bn East Yorkshire Regt   *Osnabrück*
       replaced Apr 1958 by 1st Bn Gloucestershire Regt
1st Bn Oxford and Bucks LI   *Osnabrück*
       replaced Sep 1957 by 1st Bn Duke of Cornwall's LI
7 Field Sqn RE from 26 Field Engr Regt of 4th Infantry Division

6th Armoured Division

HQ 6th Armoured Division   *Bunde*
6th Armoured Division Signal Regt   *Bunde*
27 Field Engr Regt RE   *Minden*
       1, 25 and 28 Field Sqns RE and 44 Field Park Sqn RE

HQ 20th ARMOURED BRIGADE   *Detmold*
5th R Inniskilling Dragoon Gds *Sennelager*
9th Lancers   *Detmold*
3rd Royal Tank Regt   *Detmold*
1st Bn Royal Hampshire Regt   *Lemgo*
'C' [APC] Sqn 14th/20th Hussars *Lemgo*
1st Field Regt RHA   *Munster*
      A, B, E Btys RHA [M44]
1 Field Sqn RE from 27 Field Engr Regt RE of 6th Armoured Division

---

[57] Disbanded Dec 1957.
[58] Redesignated Feb 1958 as 2nd Field Regt RA and reorganized with L, N and O Field Btys RA.
[59] Renumbered Dec 1957 as 12th Infantry Brigade.

⊡ 7ᵗʰ Armoured Division

HQ 7ᵗʰ Armoured Division   *Verden*
7ᵗʰ Armoured Division Signal Regt   *Verden*
21 Field Engr Regt RE   *Nienburg*
          4, 27, and 48 Field Sqns and 45 Field Park Sqn RE

HQ 7ᵗʰ ARMOURED BRIGADE   *Soltau*
4ᵗʰ/7ᵗʰ Dragoon Gds   *Fallingbostel*
4ᵗʰ Hussars   *Hohne*
4ᵗʰ Royal Tank Regt   *Fallingbostel*
1ˢᵗ Bn Devonshire Regt[60]   *Celle*
'A'[APC] Sqn 14ᵗʰ/20ᵗʰ Hussars *Celle*
4ᵗʰ Field Regt RHA   *Hohne*
          F, N, P Btys RHA [M44]
4 Field Sqn RE from 21 Field Engr Regt of 7ᵗʰ Armoured Division

HQ 10ᵗʰ INFANTRY BRIGADE   *Luneburg*
8ᵗʰ Hussars   *Luneburg*
1ˢᵗ Bn Welch Regt   *Luneburg*
          replaced Nov 1957 by 1ˢᵗ Bn South Staffordshire Regt
1ˢᵗ Bn Highland LI   *Luneburg*
1ˢᵗ Bn Bedfords & Herts Regt [arrived Nov 1957]   *Goslar*
6ᵗʰ Field Regt RA   *Munsterlager*
          H, V, 132 Field Btys RA [25pdr]
27 Field Sqn RE from 21 Field Engr Regt of 7ᵗʰ Armoured Division

---

[60] In May 1958 this would become 1ˢᵗ Bn Devonshire & Dorset Regt following amalgamation.

▭ *BAOR Apr 1958—Apr 1961*

HQ BAOR   *Rheindahlen*
18th Army Group Signal Regt   *Krefeld*
    redesignated Sep 1959 as 10th Signal Regt
19th Army Group Signal Regt   *St Tonis*
    redesignated Sep 1959 as 28th Signal Regt, u/c SACEUR
1st Wireless Regt   *Birgelen*
    redesignated Sep 1959 as 13th Signal Regt (Radio)
2nd L of C Signal Regt   *Düsseldorf*
    redesignated Sep 1959 as 16th Signal Regt
11th Air Formation Signal Regt   *Lemgo*
    redesignated Sep 1959 as 21st Signal Regt (Air Formation)]
12th Air Formation Signal Regt   *Lippstadt*
    redesignated Sep 1959 as 22nd Signal Regt (Air Formation)

40 Advanced Engr Stores Regt   *Willich*
    21, 46 Wkps & Park Sqns, 41 Plant Sqn RE
14 Field Survey Sqn RE   *Mönchen-Gladbach*

13th/18th Hussars [recce, AFNORTH]   *Lubbecke* [left Oct 1958]

HQ 1 Corps   *Bielefeld*
I Corps Signal Regt   *Herford*
    redesignated Sep 1959 as 7th Signal Regt (Corps)

Royal Dragoons [recce]   *Herford* [left 1959]
    replaced Jan 1960 by Life Guards
12th Lancers [recce]   *Hildesheim*
    replaced Mar 1959 by 1st Queens DG at *Wolfenbüttel*
14th/20th Hussars[61]   *Munster*
    replaced Nov 1960 by 4th Royal Tank Regt at *Hohne*

58th Medium Regt RA   *Menden* [left Dec 1958]
    118, 175 Mdm Btys RA [5.5"]

---

[61] APC regiment with one squadron each at Celle (7th Armoured Brigade Group) and Lemgo (20th Armoured Brigade Group), and one squadron with tanks in Berlin. When 4th RTR took over this role, only its RHQ was at Hohne; it had a tank squadron in Berlin ('C') and APC squadrons at Celle and Lemgo.

⊞ **1ˢᵗ AGRA (Field)** [arrived Feb 1960][62]   *Hildesheim*
24ᵗʰ Medium Regt RA   *Nienburg* [left May 1960]
      2, 51, 76 Mdm Btys RA [5.5"]
47ᵗʰ GW Regt (Field) RA [arrived 1959]   *Dortmund*
      3, 4 Btys RA [Corporal SSM]
24ᵗʰ Missile Regt RA[63] [arrived Sep 1960]   *Paderborn*
      51, 76 Btys RA [HJ rockets]; 2, 34 Btys RA [M110]
50ᵗʰ Missile Regt RA [arrived Sep 1960]*Menden*
      15, 21 Btys RA [HJ rockets]; 33, 78 Btys RA [M110]
39ᵗʰ Missile Regt RA [arrived Dec 1960]*Paderborn*
      19, 36 Btys RA [HJ rockets]; 75, 176 Btys RA [M110]
27ᵗʰ GW Regt (Field) RA [arrived 1961]   *Dortmund*
      6, 137 Btys RA [Corporal SSM]
94ᵗʰ Locating Regt RA   *Celle*
      112 Loc Bty RA[64]
218ᵗʰ Signal Sqn   *Hildesheim*

44ᵗʰ Heavy AA Regt RA   *Delmenhorst* [disbanded Mar 1959]
      116, 153, 154 HAA Btys RA
12ᵗʰ LAA Regt RA   *Lippstadt*; Oct 1958 to *Delmenhorst*
      T, 9, 34 LAA Btys RA
35ᵗʰ Light AA Regt RA   *Oldenburg* [disbanded Oct 1958]
      90, 92, 99 LAA Btys RA [40mm]

⊞ **1ˢᵗ Wing AAC**   *Detmold*
652ⁿᵈ Sqn AAC   *Detmold*
654ᵗʰ Sqn AAC   *Hildesheim*
12ᵗʰ Flt AAC [BAOR HQ Flt]   *Wildenrath*

⊞ **11 Engineer Group**   *Osnabrück*
35 Corps Engr Regt   *Osnabrück*
      16, 30, 42 Field Sqns RE
36 Corps Engr Regt   *Osnabrück* [left Dec 1959]
      20, 24, 57 Field Sqns RE

---

[62] On formation in BAOR, took over command of artillery already in Germany.
[63] This is the former 24ᵗʰ Medium Regt RA, returned with a new name and new weapons.
[64] Reorganized May 1960 with 14, 73, 152, 156 Loc Btys RA.

[11 Engineer Group]
38 Corps Engr Regt   *Osnabrück* [left Jan 1959]
     61, 62, 63 Field Sqns RE
25 Corps Engr Regt [arrived 1959]   *Osnabrück*
     37, 39, 59 Field Sqns RE
26 Armd Engr Sqn RE   *Hohne*
65 Indep Field Park Sqn RE   *Osnabrück*

☐ **2nd Division**
Division HQ   *Hilden*
2nd Division Signal Regt   *Hilden*
43 Field Park Sqn RE   *Osnabrück*

⊠ 6th Infantry Brigade Group   *Munster*
2nd Royal Tank Regt   *Munster* [left Oct 1958]
     replaced Jul 1959 by 10th Hussars
     replaced Jun 1960 by Queen's Own Hussars
1st Bn Royal Northumberland Fusiliers   *Munster*
     replaced Feb 1959 by 1st Bn Royal Leicestershire Regt
1st Bn Seaforth Highlanders   *Munster*
     replaced Dec 1960 by 1st Bn King's Shropshire LI
1st Bn Royal Irish Fusiliers   *Wuppertal* [left Oct 1958]
     replaced Feb 1959 by 1st Bn Royal Inniskilling Fusiliers
     replaced Jan 1960 by 1st Bn Loyal Regt
     replaced Nov 1960 by 1st York & Lancaster Regt
40th Field Regt RA   *Munster*
     38, 78, 137 Field Btys RA [25pdr]
2 Field Sqn RE   *Dortmund*, later *Munster*

⊠ 11th Infantry Brigade Group   *Minden*
7th Royal Tank Regt   *Hohne*
     replaced Apr 1959 by 4th Royal Tank Regt
1st Bn North Staffordshire Regt[65]   *Minden*
     replaced Jun 1959 by 1st Bn S Wales Borderers

---

[65] Effective Jan 1959, 1st Bn Staffordshire Regt, following amalgamation with 1st Bn South Staffordshire Regt.

[11th Infantry Brigade Group]
1st Bn Highland LI   *Luneburg*
         replaced Nov 1958 by 1st Bn Middlesex Regt
1st Bn Royal Lincolnshire Regt [arrived Jun 1958]   *Minden*
19th Field Regt RA   *Minden*
         25, 28, 67 Field Btys RA [25pdr]
25 Field Sqn RE   *Minden*

4th Division
Division Headquarters   *Herford*
4th Division Signal Regt   *Herford*
21 Field Park Sqn RE   *Dortmund*
         replaced by 44 Field Park Sqn RE

4th GUARDS BRIGADE GROUP   *Hubblerath*
17th/21st Lancers   *Paderborn*
         replaced Feb 1960 by 5th Royal Inniskilling Dgn Gds
1st Bn Coldstream Gds   *Hubblerath*
         replaced Nov 1958 by 1st Bn Scots Gds at *Krefeld*
         replaced Nov 1960 by 1st Bn Welsh Gds
3rd Bn Coldstream Gds   *Hubblerath*
         replaced Jan 1958 by 2nd Bn Grenadier Gds
1st Bn Kings Own Yorkshire LI   *Hubblerath*; Aug 1958 to *Hilden*
41st Field Regt RA   *Lippstadt*
         88, 105, 165 Field Btys RA [25pdr]
         replaced Mar 1961 by 49th Field Regt RA {55, 127, 143 Fd Btys RA}
29 Field Sqn RE   *Hameln*

5th INFANTRY BRIGADE GROUP   *Iserlohn*
3rd Hussars   *Munster*
         replaced Oct 1958 by Royal Scots Greys
         replaced Jul 1960 by 1st Royal Tank Regt

[5th Infantry Brigade Group]
1st Bn Queens Royal Regt   *Iserlohn*
         replaced Sep 1959 by 1st Bn Green Howards
1st Bn Royal Norfolk Regt[66]   *Iserlohn*
         replaced Mar 1960 by 1st Bn Royal Ulster Rifles
1st Bn Essex Regt[67]   *Dortmund*
         replaced Oct 1959 by 1st Bn The Buffs
         replaced Nov 1960 by 1st Bn The Loyal Regt
45th Field Regt RA   *Dortmund*
         70, 116, 176 Field Btys RA [25pdr]
5 Field Sqn RE   *Iserlohn*

20th ARMOURED BRIGADE GROUP   *Detmold*
5th R Inniskilling Dgn Gds   *Sennelgager*
         replaced Jul 1960 by 10th Hussars
9th Lancers   *Detmold*
         replaced Jul 1960 by Royal Scots Greys
3rd Royal Tank Regt   *Detmold*
'A' [APC] Sqn 14th/20th Hussars   *Lemgo*
         replaced Nov 1960 by APC sqn 4th Royal Tank Regt
1st Bn Royal Hampshire Regt   *Lemgo*
         replaced Oct 1959 by 1st Bn Argyll & Sutherland Highlanders
1st Field Regt RHA   *Hildesheim*
         A, B, E Btys RHA [M44]
1 Field Sqn RE   *Sennelager*

5th Division retitled 30 Jun 1960 as **1st Division**
Division Headquarters   *Verden*
5th Division Signal Regt   *Verden* [Jun 1960 1st Division SR]
45 Field Park Sqn RE   *Nienburg*

---

[66] In Aug 1959 amalgamated with 1st Bn Suffolk Regt to form 1st Bn 1st East Anglian Regt at this station.
[67] Amalgamated Jun 1958 with 1st Bn Bedfordshire and Hertfordshire Regt to form 1st Bn 3rd East Anglian Regt at this station.

⬚ 7th ARMOURED BRIGADE GROUP   *Soltau*

4th/7th Dragoon Gds   *Fallingbostel*
    replaced Nov 1959 by 5th Royal Tank Regt
4th Hussars[68]   *Hohne*
4th Royal Tank Regt   *Fallingbostel*
    replaced Nov 1960 by 14th/20th Hussars
8th Royal Tank Regt [arrived Jan 1959]   *Fallingbostel* [left Jul 1960]
'C' [APC] sqn 14th/20th Hussars   *Celle*
    replaced Nov 1960 by 'C' [APC] Sqn 4th Royal Tank Regt
1st Bn Devonshire & Dorset Regt[69]   *Celle*
    replaced Nov 1958 by 1st Bn Gordon Highlanders
4th Field Regt RHA   *Hohne*
    F, G, I Btys RHA [M44]
4 Field Sqn RE   *Fallingbostel*

⊠ 12th INFANTRY BRIGADE GROUP   *Osnabrück*

3rd Carabiniers   *Osnabrück*
    replaced Apr 1959 by 16th/5th Lancers
1st Bn King's Regt   *Osnabrück* [left May 1958]
    replaced Jan 1959 by 1st Bn 1st Green Jackets
1st Bn Gloucestershire Regt   *Osnabrück*
    replaced Jan 1960 by 1st Bn Lancashire Fusiliers
1st Bn Duke of Cornwall's LI[70]   *Osnabrück*
6th Field Regt RA   *Munsterlager*
    H, V, 132 Field Btys RA [25pdr]
7 Field Sqn RE   *Osnabrück*

---

[68] 4th Hussars amalgamated Oct 1958 at this station with 8th Hussars to form Queen's Royal Irish Hussars.
[69] 1st Bn Devonshire Regt at this station amalgamated May 1958 with 1st Bn Dorset Regt to form 1st Bn Devonshire & Dorset Regt.
[70] Amalgamated Oct 1959 with 1st Bn Somerset LI to form 1st Bn Somerset & Cornwall LI at this station.

☐ *BAOR Apr 1961—Apr 1964*

HQ BAOR   *Rheindahlen*
10th Signal Regt   *Krefeld* [left Apr 1962]
13th Signal Regt (Radio)   *Birgelen*
16th Signal Regt   *Krefeld*
21st Signal Regt (Air Formation)   *Lemgo*
28th Signal Regt   *St Tonis*

40 Advanced Engr Stores Regt   *Wilich*
        21, 46 Wkps & Pk Sqns, 41 Plant Sqn RE
14 Field Survey Sqn RE   *Mönchen-Gladbach*

HQ 1 Corps   *Bielefeld*
7th Signal Regt (Corps)   *Herford*
22nd Signal Regt (Corps)   *Lippstadt*
18 Flight AAC [1 Corps HQ Flt]   *Detmold*

Life Guards [recce]   *Herford*
        replaced Oct 1962 by Royal Horse Guards
1st Queens Dgn Gds [recce]   *Wolfenbüttel*
4th Royal Tank Regt [APC regt][71]   *Hohne* [role discontinued Aug 1963]

☐ **1st Artillery Brigade (Field)**[72]   *Hildesheim*
27th Regt RA (GW)   *Dortmund*
        6, 137 Btys RA [GW Field: Corporal SSM]
47th Regt RA (GW)   *Dortmund*
        3. 4 Btys RA [GW Field: Corporal SSM]
32nd Regt RA[73] [arrived Jan 1962]   *Dortmund* [left Jan 1964]
21st Locating Regt RA[74] [arrived Jan 1962]   *Fallingbostel* [left Jun 1964]
        7, 20, 57 Loc Btys RA

---

[71] The regiment had one APC squadron at Celle and another at Lemgo with 7th and 20th Armoured Brigades, respectively, along with a tank squadron in Berlin.
[72] 1st AGRA (Field) redesignated 1st Artillery Brigade (Field) on 4 Oct 1961.
[73] Roled as "atomic delivery regiment"; presumably holding and guarding nuclear warheads. Became a support regiment (later general support regiment) officially 1 Jan 1962. Re-roled as a medium regiment Mar 1964 after leaving BAOR.
[74] A medium regiment converted to locating role; 20 Bty RA placed in suspended animation 31 Oct 1961 and 7 Loc Bty RA placed in suspended animation 30 Nov 1961; 156 Loc Bty RA joined 31 Oct 1961 and 14 Loc Bty RA on 23 Jan 1962 (both from 94th Locating Regt RA). 57 Loc Bty RA went to 94th Locating Regt RA 29 Apr 1964.

[1st Artillery Brigade (Field)]
94 Locating Regt RA[75]   *Celle*
      14, 73, 152, 156 Loc Btys RA
15th/19th Hussars[76] [arrived Sep 1961]   *Munster*
218 Signal Sqn   *Hildesheim*

⬠ **7th Artillery Brigade (AA)** [arrived Sep 1961][77]   *Gütersloh*
36th Regt RA (GW)[78]   [arrived Sep 1961] *Gütersloh*, then *Duisburg* Nov-Dec
      56, 60 Btys RA [GW AA: Thunderbird SAM]
12th LAA Regt RA   *Delmenhorst*
      T, 9, 34 LAA Btys RA [40mm]
      replaced May 1963 by 22nd LAA Regt RA at *Gütersloh* {47, 48, 53
          LAA Btys RA}
16th LAA Regt RA [arrived 1962]   *Krefeld*
      30, 32 LAA Btys RA[40mm]
34th LAA Regt RA [arrived Oct 1963]   *Wuppertal*
      11, 49, 58 LAA Btys RA [40mm]
217th Signal Sqn   *Gütersloh*

▭ **1st Wing AAC**   *Detmold*
652nd Sqn AAC {1, 9 Flts}   *Detmold*
654th Sqn AAC {4, 5 Flts [also 17 & 22 Flts?]}   *Hildesheim*
655th Sqn AAC {23, 24 Flts}   *Detmold*
12th Flt AAC [BAOR HQ Flt]   *Wildenrath*

▥ **11 Engineer Gp**   *Osnabrück*
25 Cops Engr Regt   *Osnabrück*
      37, 39,59 Field Sqns RE
35 Corps Engr Regt   *Osnabrück*
      16, 30, 42 Field Sqns RE
65 Indep Field Park Sqn RE   *Osnabrück*
28 Amphibious Engr Sqn [arrived late 1962]   *Hameln*

---

[75] Transferred 14 and 156 Loc Btys RA to 21st Locating Regt RA (23 Jan 1962 and 31 Oct 1961, respectively). Gained 57 Loc Bty RA from that regiment 29 Apr 1964.
[76] Tasked as nuclear escort regiment.
[77] 7th AGRA (AA) redesignated 7th Artillery Brigade (AA) 4 Oct 1961.
[78] Redesignated Mar 1964 as 36th Hy AD Regt RA.

□ 1st **Division**
Division HQ   *Verden*
1st Division Signal Regt   *Verden*
39th Missile Regt RA   *Paderborn*
          19, 36 Btys RA [HJ rocket] and 75, 171 Btys RA [M110].
26 Armoured Engr Sqn RE   *Hohne*
45 Field Park Sqn RE   *Nienburg*

□ 7th ARMOURED BRIGADE GROUP   *Soltau*
207 Signal Sqn   *Soltau*
Queen's Royal Irish Hussars   *Fallingbostel* [left Jun 1961]
        replaced Jan 1962 by 14th/20th Hussars
        replaced Jul 1962 by 11th Hussars
13th/18th Hussars   *Hohne*
5th Royal Tank Regt   *Fallingbostel*
APC sqn 4th Royal Tank Regt   *Celle* [left Aug 1963]
1st Bn Gordon Highlanders   *Celle*
        replaced Jan 1962 by 1st Bn Royal Irish Fusiliers
4th Regt RHA   *Hohne*
        F, G, I Btys RHA [M44]
        replaced Jun 1961 by 25th Regt RA {35, 54, 93 Field Btys RA}
4 Field Sqn RE   *Fallingbostel*

□ 20th ARMOURED BRIGADE GROUP   *Detmold*
200 Signal Sqn   *Detmold*
Royal Scots Greys   *Detmold*
        replaced Oct 1962 by 4th/7th Dragoon Gds
3rd Royal Tank Regt   *Detmold*
        replaced Jul 1962 by 3rd Carabiniers
Queens Own Hussars [arrived Aug 1962]   *Detmold*
        Replaced Mar 1964 by 17th/21st Lancers
APC sqn 4th Royal Tank Regt   *Lemgo* [left Aug 1963]
1st Bn Argyll & Sutherland Highlanders   *Lemgo*
        replaced Jan 1962 by 1st Bn Royal Northumberland Fusiliers
1st Regt RHA   *Hildesheim*
        A, B, E Btys RHA [M144 SP]
1 Field Sqn RE   *Nienburg*

☐** **2ⁿᵈ Division**

Division HQ   *Lubbecke*
2ⁿᵈ Division Signal Regt   *Lubbecke*
24ᵗʰ Missile Regt RA   *Paderborn*
        51, 76 Btys RA [HJ rocket] and 2, 34 Btys RA [M110]
43 Field Park Sqn RE   *Osnabrück*

⊠* 6ᵗʰ Iɴꜰᴀɴᴛʀʏ Bʀɪɢᴀᴅᴇ Gʀᴏᴜᴘ   *Munster*
206 Signal Sqn   *Munster*
Queen's Own Hussars   *Munster*
        replaced Aug 1962 by 4ᵗʰ/7ᵗʰ Dragoon Gds
1ˢᵗ Bn Royal Leicestershire Regt   *Munster*
        replaced Nov 1961 by 1ˢᵗ Bn Cheshire Regt
1ˢᵗ Bn King's Shropshire LI   *Munster*
        replaced Nov 1963 by 1ˢᵗ Bn Queens R Surrey Regt
1ˢᵗ Bn York & Lancaster Regt   *Munster*
        replaced Nov 1962 by 1ˢᵗ Bn Royal Hampshire Regt
40ᵗʰ Regt RA [Field]   *Munster*
        38, 78, 137 Field Btys RA [25pdr]
2 Field Sqn RE   *Munster*

⊠* 11ᵗʰ Iɴꜰᴀɴᴛʀʏ Bʀɪɢᴀᴅᴇ Gʀᴏᴜᴘ   *Bad Lippspringe*
211 Signal Sqn   *Bad Lippspringe*
14ᵗʰ/20ᵗʰ Hussars   *Fallingbostel*
        replaced Jun 1962 by 1ˢᵗ Royal Tank Regt
        replaced Feb 1964 by Royal Scots Greys
1ˢᵗ Bn Cameronians [joined 1961]   *Minden* [left Apr 1964]
1ˢᵗ Bn Middlesex Regt   *Minden*
        replaced Apr 1962 by 1ˢᵗ Bn Royal Warwickshire Regt at *Hameln*;
                1964 to *Minden*
1ˢᵗ Bn South Wales Borderers   *Minden*
        replaced Nov 1962 by 1ˢᵗ Bn Worcestershire Regt
19ᵗʰ Regt RA [Field]   *Bad Lippspringe*
        25, 28, 67 Field Btys RA [25pdr]
25 Field Sqn RE   *Paderborn*

⊠* 12ᵗʰ Iɴꜰᴀɴᴛʀʏ Bʀɪɢᴀᴅᴇ Gʀᴏᴜᴘ   *Osnabrück*
212 Signal Sqn   *Osnabrück*
16ᵗʰ/5ᵗʰ Lancers   *Osnabrück*
        replaced Jan 1964 by 9ᵗʰ/12ᵗʰ Lancers

[12th Infantry Brigade Group]
1st Bn Somerset & Cornwall LI   *Osnabrück*
        replaced May 1961 by 1st Bn 2nd East Anglian Regt [left Mar 1964]
1st Bn Lancashire Fusiliers   *Osnabrück*
1st Bn POWO Regt of Yorkshire   *Osnabrück*
        replaced Jun 1963 by 1st Bn Royal Fusiliers
6th Regt RA [Field]   *Osnabrück*
        H, V, 132 Field Btys RA [25pdr]
        replaced Aug 1962 by 18th Regt RA [Field] {18, 40, 52 Field Btys RA}
7 Field Sqn RE   *Osnabrück*

4th Division
Division HQ   *Herford*
4th Division Signal Regt   *Herford*
50th Missile Regt RA   *Menden*
        5, 21 Btys RA [HJ rocket] and 33, 78 Btys RA [M110]
44 Field Park Sqn RE   *Paderborn*

4th GUARDS BRIGADE GROUP   *Hubblerath*
204 Signal Sqn   *Hubblerath*
5th Royal Inniskilling Dragoon Guards   *Munster* [left Oct 1962]
        replaced Mar 1963 by 17th/21st Lancers
        replaced Jan 1964 by 13th/18th Hussars
2nd Bn Coldstream Gds   *Hubblerath*
        replaced Nov 1961 by 1st Bn Irish Gds
1st Bn Welsh Gds   *Hubblerath*
        replaced Nov 1963 by 1st Bn Grenadier Gds
1st Bn KO Yorkshire LI   *Hilden*
        replaced Aug 1961 by 1st Bn Lancashire Regt
        replaced Jan 1964 by 1st Bn Royal Highland Fusiliers at *Iserlohn*
49th Regt RA [Field]   *Dortmund*
        55, 127, 143 Field Btys RA [25pdr]
        replaced May 1963 by 14th Regt RA [Field] {1, 5, 13 Field Btys RA}
29 Field Sqn RE   *Hameln*

✉ 5th INFANTRY BRIGADE GROUP[79]   *Iserlohn*

205 Signal Sqn   *Iserlohn*

1st Royal Tank Regt   *Munster*; Sep 1961 to *Hohne*
    replaced Jan 1962 by 10th Hussars

1st Bn Green Howards   *Dortmund*
    replaced Feb 1963 by 1st Bn Royal Highland Fusiliers at *Iserlohn*

1st Bn Loyal Regt   *Wuppertal*
    replaced Jun 1962 by 1st Bn KOR Border Regt

1st Bn Royal Ulster Rifles   *Iserlohn*
    replaced Apr 1963 by 1st Bn Royal Welch Fusiliers

45th Regt RA [Field]   *Minden*
    70, 116, 176 Field Btys RA [25pdr]
    replaced May 1963 by 14th Regt RA [Field] {1, 3, 13 Field Btys RA}

5 Field Sqn RE   *Iserlohn*

---

[79] 5th Infantry Brigade HQ was withdrawn to the UK in Apr 1964.

⊠ 4th CANADIAN INFANTRY BRIGADE GROUP

Note: the Canadian brigade in Europe. The Canadian NATO contribution had been raised in 1951 as 27th Canadian Infantry Brigade Group, sailing to Germany in Nov and Dec of that year. It was placed under BAOR on arrival and moved to the Hanover area, settling at CFB[Canadian Forces Base] Soest. This was a conventional infantry brigade group (three infantry battalions, armoured squadron, field artillery regiment, field engineer squadron, and supporting units) formed from volunteers from reserve regiments. It was replaced Oct 1953 by the 1st Canadian Infantry Brigade Group, an Active Force unit with a battalion from each of the three regular infantry regiments (Royal Canadian Regiment, Princess Patricia's Canadian Light Infantry, and Royal 22^e Regiment), an armoured squadron (from Lord Strathcona's Horse), artillery (regular Canadian artillery were designated as regiments RCHA), engineers, etc. In 1955, the 2nd Canadian Infantry Brigade Group came to Europe to replace the 1st. Finally, in Nov 1957 the 4th Canadian Infantry Brigade Group came over and replaced the 2nd.[80]

The 4th had a full armoured regiment, as well as a recce squadron, in addition to the three infantry battalions and other elements. From that point, the Canadians stopped rotating entire brigades, but did rotate armoured regiments and infantry battalions.[81] In 1962 they added light helicopters which would ultimately (ca. 1968) become No. 444 Squadron RCAF [CH-112 Nomad and CH-136 Kiowa helicopters].[82] The brigade's peak strength was just over 6700 men in the mid 1960s. As with the British, the infantry battalions came to be mechanised and on 1 May 1968 the brigade was redesignated 4th Canadian Mechanised Brigade Group. It left BAOR and relocated to Lahr in southern Germany Jun 1971, after which it was gradually reduced in strength. It closed out in Europe in 1993.

---

[80] 4th Canadian Infantry Brigade Group had been formed in 1950 as the 25th and sent to Korea. It closed down there in Dec 1954 and reopened in Canada as the 4th in Feb 1955.
[81] The three armoured regiments were the Royal Canadian Dragoons, Lord Strathcona's Horse, and 8th Canadian Hussars. Lord Strathcona's are known to have been the armoured regiment 1966-70.
[82] The brigade had been redesignated as mechanised when the squadron formed. Until disbanded in 1967 No. 444 had been a CF-104 Starfighter squadron in Germany.

⌗ *BAOR Apr 1964—Dec 1970*

HQ BAOR   *Rheindahlen*
HQ 4th Signal Group [formed Oct 1969]   *Rheindahlen*
    13th Signal Regt (Radio)   *Birgelen*
    16th Signal Regt   *Krefeld*
    21st Signal Regt (Air Formation)   *Lemgo*
    28th Signal Regt   *St Tonis*

40 Advanced Engr Stores Regt   *Wilich*
    2, 46 Wksp Sqns, 41 Plant Sqn RE
14 Topographic Sqn RE   *Mönchen-Gladbach*

HQ 1 Corps   *Bielefeld*
7th Signal Regt   *Herford*
22nd Signal Regt   *Lippstadt*

Royal Horse Guards [recce]   *Herford*
    replaced Jun 1966 by 4th Royal Tank Regt
    replaced Jan 1968 by 5th Royal Inniskilling DG
1st Queen's Dragoon Guards [recce]   *Wolfenbüttel*
    replaced Jun 1964 by Queens Royal Irish Hussars [left Jan 1968]
    replaced Jun 1968 by 5th Royal Tank Regt
    replaced Dec 1969 by 3rd Royal Tank Regt

⊡ **1st Artillery Brigade (Field)**   *Hildesheim*
27th Army Missile Regt RA   *Dortmund* [withdrawn Oct 1965]
    6, 137 Btys RA [Corporal SSM]
47th Army Missile Regt RA   *Dortmund* [withdrawn Jan 1967]
    3, 4 Btys RA [Corporal SSM]
32nd Heavy Regt RA [assigned Apr 1965]   *Hildesheim*
    46, 50, 74 Hy Btys RA [M107]
20th Heavy Regt RA [assigned Jan 1966]   *Fallingbostel*
    12, 27, 43 Hy Btys RA [M107]
94th Locating Regt RA   *Celle*
    14, 73, 152, 156 Loc Btys RA[83]

---

[83] Reduced Mar ,1964 to 73 and 152 Loc Btys RA and reorganized 1965 with 73 and 57 Loc Btys RA.

[1st Artillery Brigade (Field)]
21st Locating Regt RA[present Mar-Jun 1964 only] *Fallingbostel*
14, 20, 156 Loc Btys RA
10th Hussars [assigned Aug 1965: nuclear escort][84] *Munster*
replaced Sep 1969 by 3rd Carabiniers
218 Signal Sqn *Hildesheim*

7th Artillery Brigade (AA) *Gütersloh*
36th HyAD Regt RA *Duisburg*; moved 1966 to *Dortmund* [left Apr 1968]
56, 60 HAD Btys RA [Thunderbird SAM]
16th LtAD Regt RA *Krefeld* [left Mar 1965]
30, 32 LtAD Btys RA [40mm]
22nd LtAD Regt RA *Hubblerath*
42, 53 LtAD Btys RA [40mm Bofors]
replaced Mar 1966 by 12th LAD Regt RA {T, 9 LtAD Btys RA}[85]
replaced Jun 1970 by 22nd LtAD regt RA {11, 42, 53 LtAD Btys RA}
34th LtAD Regt RA[86] *Wuppertal*; moved 1965 to *Hilden*, 1967 *Dortmund* [left Feb 1969]
11, 58 LtAD Btys RA [40mm]
217th Signal Sqn *Hildesheim*

HQ 1 Wing/HQ Army Aviation *Detmold*
12th Flt AAC [BAOR HQ Flt] *Wildenrath*
18th Flt AAC [HQ 1 Corps Flt] *Detmold*

11 Engineer Gp *Osnabrück* [disbanded 1969]
25 Corps Engr Regt[87] *Osnabrück*
12, 37, 50 Field Sqns RE
35 Corps Engr Regt[88] *Osnabrück*
29, 30, 42 Field Sqns RE
65 Corps Field Pk Sqn RE *Osnabrück*

---

[84] 8th Regiment RCT, established in 1965, had actual responsibility for transport and safe custody of nuclear warheads, with the armoured regiments serving as armed escort.
[85] Added 58th LAA Bty RA (ex 34th LAA Regt RA) 1 Jan 1970.
[86] Regiment placed in suspended animation 31 Dec 1969 and batteries transferred to 12th and 22nd LAA Regts RA.
[87] Regiment reorganized Apr 1969 and assigned to 2nd Division.
[88] Regiment reorganized Apr 1969 and assigned to 4th Division.

32 Armd Engr Regt[89]   *Hohne*
      2 and 26 Armd Engr Sqns RE
23 Amphib Sqn RE   *Hameln*

▢** 1st Division

1st Division HQ and Signal Regiment   *Verden*
1st Division Aviation[90] {9, 17, 26 Flts AAC}   *Detmold*
39th Missile Regt RA[91]   *Paderborn*
      19, 36 Btys RA [HJ rocket] and 75, 171 Btys RA [M110].
1st Regt RHA   *Hildesheim*
      A, B, E Btys RHA [25pdr]
      replaced Sep 1965 by 26th Field Regt RA {16, 17, 159 Field Btys RA}
              at *Hohne*
18th Field Regt RA   *Munsterlager*
      18, 40, 52 Field Btys RA [25pdr]
      replaced Sep 1966 by 4th Field Regt RA {29, 88, 97 Field Btys RA
              [Abbot]}
25th Field Regt RA   *Hohne*
      35, 54, 93 Field Btys RA [M44]
      replaced Dec 1965 by 45th Med Regt RA {70, 170, 176 Mdm Btys RA
              [M109]} at *Paderborn*
1st Division RE   *Nienburg*
      1, 4 Field Sqns and 45 Field Pk Sqn RE
{1st Division RE reorganized Apr 1969 as 21 Engineer Regt (1 and 4 Field
Sqns RE) at Nienburg, 32 Armd Engr Regt[92] (30 and 37 Field Sqns RE) at
Hohne, 26 Armd Engr Sqn at Hohne, and 45 Field Pk Sqn RE at Nienburg}

▢* 7th Armoured Brigade   *Soltau*

207 Signal Sqn   *Soltau*
11th Hussars   *Hohne*
      replaced Jan 1969 by 1st Bn Green Howards at *Minden*
1st Royal Tank Regt   *Fallingbostel*
      replaced Dec 1965 by 2nd Royal Tank Regt at *Hohne*
      replaced Jul 1970 by Queen's Own Hussars

---

[89] Reorganized Apr 1969 and made part of 1st Division RE.
[90] Reorganized Oct 1969 as 1st Regiment AAC (651, 657 and 658 Sqns AAC).
[91] 75 Bty RA replaced May 1968 by H Bty RA.
[92] Although allowed to retain its former designation, 32 Armoured Engineer Regt was
now just a conventional field engineer regiment.

[7th Armoured Brigade]
5th Royal Tank Regt   *Fallingbostel*
       replaced Feb 1965 by 3rd Royal Tank Regt at *Hohne*
       replaced Jan 1968 by 4th Royal Tank Regt
1st Bn Royal Irish Fusiliers   *Celle*
       replaced Sep 1965 by 1st Bn Royal Anglian Regt
       replaced Mar 1968 by 3rd Bn Royal Green Jackets
       replaced 1970 by 1st Bn Royal Green Jackets

⊠ 11th INFANTRY BRIGADE[93] *Minden*
211 Signal Sqn   *Minden*
Royal Scots Greys   *Fallingbostel*
1st Bn Royal Warwickshire Fusiliers   *Minden*
       replaced Jun 1966 by 1st Bn Duke of Edinburgh's Royal Regt
       replaced Jun 1969 by 16th/5th Lancers at *Fallingbostel*
1st Bn Royal Welch Fusiliers [assigned Mar 1964]   *Minden*
       replaced Apr 1967 by 1st Gordon Highlanders
       replaced Nov 1969 by 15th/19th Hussars t *Fallingbostel*
1st Bn Black Watch [assigned Mar 1964]`   *Minden*
       replaced Mar 1968 by 1st Bn Sherwood Foresters at *Lubbecke*
         [left 1970]

□ 2nd **Division**
2nd Division HQ and Signal Regiment   *Lubbecke*
2nd Division Aviation {4, 5, 27 Flts AAC}[94]   *Hildesheim*
50th Missile Regt RA[95]   *Menden*
       15, 21 Btys RA [HJ rockets] and 33, 78 Btys RA [M110].
5th Field Regt RA [assigned Jun 1964]   *Gütersloh*
       K, P, Q Field Btys RA [Abbot]
       replaced Jul 1969 by 40th Field Regt RA {29, 38, 137 Field Btys RA}
42nd Medium Regt RA   *Lippstadt* [left Feb 1969]
       49, 68, 94 Mdm Btys RA [5.5"; M109 from Jun 1967]
2nd Division RE[96]   *Osnabrück*
       7, 16 Field Sqns and 43 Field Pk Sqn RE

---

[93] Redesignated by the end of 1970 as 11th Armoured Brigade.
[94] Reorganized Oct 1969 as 2nd Regt AAC (652, 659 and 660 Sqns AAC).
[95] In Mar 1968, 56 Bty replaced 78 Bty.
[96] 2 Field Sqn RE left Sep 1964; 29 Field Sqn RE left in 1964; 16 Field Sqn RE joined division RE in 1964; and 73 Field Sqn RE was assigned 1968-69. 7 Field Sqn RE moved to Ripon, UK in Feb 1968.

[2ⁿᵈ Division]
{2ⁿᵈ Division RE reorganized Apr 1969 as 23 Engineer Regt (7 and 16 Field Sqns RE), 25 Engineer Regt (12 and 39 Field Sqns RE), 31 Armd Engr Sqn, and 43 Field Pk Sqn RE; all at *Osnabrück*}

⊠ 6ᵗʰ INFANTRY BRIGADE   *Munster*[97]
206 Signal Sqn   *Minden*
15ᵗʰ/19ᵗʰ Hussars   *Munster*
        replaced Mar 1968 by 4ᵗʰ/7ᵗʰ Dragoon Guards at *Sennelager*
        replaced Nov 1970 by Queen's Royal Irish Hussars
1ˢᵗ Bn Queens Royal Surrey Regt[98]   *Munster* [relieved Jan 1968]
1ˢᵗ Bn Royal Fusiliers   *Munster* [left 1967]
1ˢᵗ Bn Cheshire Regt   *Munster*
        relieved Jun 1966 by 1ˢᵗ Bn Sherwood Foresters at *Lubbecke*
            [left Mar 1968]

⊠ 12ᵗʰ INFANTRY BRIGADE[99]   *Osnabrück*
212 Signal Sqn   *Osnabrück*
9ᵗʰ/12ᵗʰ Lancers   *Osnabrück*
        replaced Mar 1969 by 1ˢᵗ Royal Tank Regt
1ˢᵗ Bn KOR Border Regt   *Osnabrück*
        replaced Dec 1965 by 1ˢᵗ Bn Devonshire & Dorset Regt
        replaced Jun 1970 by 1ˢᵗ Bn Queen's Lancashire Regt
1ˢᵗ Bn Duke of Wellington's Regt   *Osnabrück*
        replaced May 1967 by 1ˢᵗ Bn KO Scottish Borderers
1ˢᵗ Bn QO Highlanders   *Osnabrück*
        replaced Nov 1966 by 1ˢᵗ Bn Royal Scots
        replaced Jan 1970 by -1ˢᵗ Bn Royal Regt of Wales

---

[97] 6ᵗʰ Infantry Brigade (except for the tank regiment) was withdrawn to the UK in Mar 1968; initial station unclear, but it was at Barnard Castle by 1970.
[98] Battalion redesignated Dec 1966 as 1ˢᵗ Bn Queen's Regt.
[99] The brigade was largely reorganized Mar-Apr 1964 with new infantry battalions, although 1ˢᵗ Bn King's Shropshire LI at Osnabrück lingered to Jun 1964. By the end of 1970 it was redesignated as 12ᵗʰ Mechanised Brigade.

⬚ **4th Division**

4th Division HQ and Signal Regiment   *Herford*
4th Division Aviation{1, 23, 24 Flts AAC}[100]   *Detmold*
24th Missile Regt RA   *Paderborn*
        51, 76 Btys RA [HJ rockets] and 2, 34 Btys RA [M110]
14th Field Regt RA   *Dortmund*
        1, 5, 13 Field Btys RA [25pdr]
        replaced Jun 1967 by 19th Field Regt RA {25, 28, 67 Field Btys RA
            [Abbot]}
49th Field Regt RA   *Hubblerath*
        58, 127, 143 Field Btys RA [25pdr]
        replaced Mar 1965 by 3rd Regt RHA {C, D, J Btys RHA [Abbot]}
        replaced May 1970 by 1st Regt RHA {A, B, E Btys RHA}
27th Medium Regt RA [assigned Jan 1969]   *Lippstadt*
        6, 132, 137 Mdm Btys RA [M109]
4th Division RE   *Paderborn*
        5, 25 Field Sqns and 44 Field Pk Sqn RE
{4th Division RE reorganized Apr 1969 as 26 Engineer Regt (5 and 25 Field
Sqns RE), 35 Engr Regt (29 and 42 Field Sqns RE), 2 Armd Engr Sqn, and 44
Field Pk Sqn RE; all at *Paderborn*}

✉ 4th GUARDS BRIGADE[101]   *Iserlohn*; to *Munster* Mar 1968
204 Signal Sqn   *Iserlohn*; to *Munster* Mar 1968
13th/18th Hussars   *Munster*
        replaced Sep 1967 by 14th/20th Hussars
        replaced Jan 1970 by 5th Royal Inniskilling DG
1st Bn Grenadier Gds   *Iserlohn*
        replaced Apr 1966 by 2nd Bn Grenadier Gds
        replaced Jan 1969 by 2nd Bn Coldstream Gds at *Munster*
1st Bn Irish Gds   *Hubblerath*
        replaced Jul 1964 by 1st Bn Coldstream Gds at *Iserlohn*
        replaced Feb 1967 by 2nd Bn Scots Gds at *Munster*
        replaced Mar 1970 by 1st Bn Welsh Gds
1st Bn Royal Highland Fusiliers   *Iserlohn*
        replaced Apr 1967 by 2nd Bn Royal Green Jackets at *Munster*
        replaced Apr 1969 by 14th/20th Hussars at *Paderborn*
        replaced 1970 by 13th/18th Hussars at *Munster*

---

[100] Reorganized Oct 1969 as 4th Regt AAC (654, 661 and 662 Sqns AAC).
[101] Redesignated 4th Armoured Brigade by the end of 1970.

▭ 20th ARMOURED BRIGADE   *Detmold*

200 Signal Sqn   *Detmold*

3rd Carabiniers   *Detmold*
     replaced Nov 1967 by 1st Queens Dragoon Gds

4th/7th Dragoon Gds   *Detmold*
     replaced Feb 1965 by Royal Dragoons[102]

17th/21st Lancers   *Detmold*
     replaced Jul 1969 by 2nd Bn Royal Green Jackets at *Munster*
     replaced Dec 1970 by 3rd Bn Royal Anglian Regt at *Paderborn*

1st Bn Royal Northumberland Fusiliers   *Lemgo*
     replaced Mar 1966 by 1st Bn Royal Sussex Regt[103]
     replaced Apr 1970 by -1st Bn Light Infantry

---

[102] Regiment amalgamated Feb 1969 with Royal Horse Guards at this station to form Blues and Royals.

[103] Battalion redesignated Dec 1966 as 3rd Bn Queen's Regt.

The 1970s: Reorganizations

While its cantonments across northern Germany—with barracks, housing for wives and children, schools, NAAFI stores, and other trappings of normal British military bases—might seem like similar garrisons in Great Britain, there was one significant difference. BAOR was theoretically an army that could go to war with little notice.

As part of Britain's contribution to NATO, their purpose was to deter further Soviet aggression or, failing that to fight against a Soviet invasion. Scholars and officers wrestled with a number of issues from the 1950s to the 1980s: whether a conventional defence against the much larger Soviet forces and their thousands of tanks was even possible; if the troops were intended merely to be trip wires (providing a pause on the ground before massive retaliation); the possible uses of tactical nuclear weapons (and later, of chemical weapons). However unlikely a Soviet attack might have been, crises all through the Cold War years (the Hungarian revolt of 1956, the Berlin Wall in 1961, the 1968 Czech uprising) served as a reminder of why British and other troops were stationed in West Germany. Perforce, the Army had to plan for armoured warfare under conditions where nuclear or chemical weapons might be employed. Readiness and doctrine were tested by periodic alerts and exercises, although during some periods at least the latter might not have actually provided useful training.[104]

Formations

At the beginning of this period, the three divisions had six brigades, with a total of 11 armoured regiments and 13 mechanised infantry battalions among them. Divisions had one or two regiments with the Abbot 105mm SP gun (for close support of a brigade) and one with the M109 155mm SP howitzer. The aviation component was a regiment AAC with three squadrons. Divisional RE was organized into two regiments (each of two field squadrons), an armoured engineer squadron and a field support squadron. There were two armoured car

---

[104] "Much of the deliberate gamesmanship, even trickery, during BAOR exercises—and particularly Command Post exercises—had been exposed between 1977 and 1983. 'Everyone cheated and everyone knew they did,' recorded General Sir John Walters, '…it was not training for war.'" Patrick Mileham, "Fifty Years of British Army Officership 1960—2010, Part II: Prospective" *Defense & Security Analysis*, Jun 2004 (Vol 20, No 2), 180. As with the US Army at about the same time, the British would re-think their doctrine and improve their training. For both armies, the results would be seen—not in Central Europe, ironically—but in the first Gulf War.

regiments in 1 Corps for reconnaissance and screening.[105] The wheeled APCs had been replaced by the tracked FV432. The Chieftain tank was replacing the old Centurion and the Army was looking to replace the old Saladin armoured cars with a new family of tracked reconnaissance vehicles. BAOR was now around 55,000 or 56,000 personnel.

In Mar 1971 the newly-returned 6th Armoured Brigade was assigned to 4th Division, which then shifted 4th Armoured Brigade to the 2nd Division, which had retained control of the 6th while the brigade had been in England. At this point, the assignments were:

1st Division	Verden
7th Armoured Brigade	Soltau
11th Armoured Brigade	Minden
2nd Division	Lubbecke
4th Armoured Brigade	Munster
12th Mechanised Brigade	Osnabrück
4th Division	Herford
6th Armoured Brigade	Soest[106]
20th Armoured Brigade	Detmold

A detailed order of battle for BAOR 1971—76 begins below at page 79.

Towards the end of the decade, BAOR underwent a major restructuring. 2nd Division began experimenting with a new organization during 1976. It would complete testing and be reorganized between Sep 1976 and Mar 1977 as 2nd Armoured Division. The three divisions and six brigades disappeared, reorganized into four divisions (1st, 2nd, 3rd and 4th Armoured), each with two task force headquarters, and the brigade-sized 5th Field Force. 1st and 4th Divisions became 1st and 4th Armoured Divisions under the new organization later in 1977. 3rd Division, which had been in the UK, appeared 1 Jan 1978 in Germany (headquarters at Korbecke, near Soest) as 3rd Armoured Division.

The detailed order of battle for BAOR 1977—1980 begins below at page 87.

Each division had two armoured regiments, intended to have 74 tanks each. At full strength, these new large regiments would be almost equal to the old

---

[105] Reductions 1969 and 1971 brought armour down to 19 regiments, so BAOR's 13 formed 68-percent of that arm.
[106] Actually, at Korbecke (near Soest), but it is more often shown as at Soest.

armoured brigade's total of 94 tanks in two regiments.[107] The division also had
three mechanised infantry battalions and an armoured recce regiment with the
new tracked family of recce vehicles. The FV438 vehicles with Swingfire
ATGM came out of the armoured regiments into an independent RHA
battery.[108] Artillery comprised one regiment with the Abbot SP 105mm (24
tubes) and a mixed regiment with the M109 SP 155mm (12 tubes) and M110
SP 203mm [US 8"] (4 tubes), along with an air defence battery with the
Blowpipe SAM. The division also had an engineer field regiment, a regiment
of the Army Air Corps (15 Lynx AH and 16 utility helicopters), and other
supporting units. The field force had three motorised infantry battalions, an
armoured recce regiment, and a regiment with FH70 towed 155mm howitzers.
This gave BAOR 8 armoured and 5 armoured recce regiments (versus the old
structure with 11 armoured and 2 armoured car regiments) and 15 infantry
battalions (an increase of 2 battalions). The old screen force disappeared, and
all recce regiments were now part of divisions.

The task force headquarters were designated sequentially through the divisions,
Alpha through Hotel. Task forces could command any grouping of units from
the division; unlike the former brigades, they did not have units directly
assigned to them. The expectation was that the five maneuver units (two
armoured regiments and three mechanised battalions) would be organized into
five cross-functional combat teams. The 24th Infantry Brigade, at Catterick,
was redesignated as 5th Field Force and moved to BOAR.[109]

1st Armoured Division	Verden
TF Alpha	Soltau
TF Bravo	Hohne
2nd Armoured Division	Lubbecke
TF Charlie	Munster
TF Delta	Osnabrück

---

[107] It seems unlikely, given what we know of manning and equipment levels at various
periods, that either the new regiments or old brigades were ever at full strength in
peacetime.

[108] These vehicles transferred to the Royal Artillery, thus returning the anti-tank role
transferred from the RA to the RAC in 1950. The 3rd Regiment RHA was broken up
and its C, D, and J Batteries RHA formed three of the new units; M Battery RHA was
reformed as the fourth. Since 3rd RHA had served in an anti-tank role in the Western
Desert early in World War II, their selection might not have been a coincidence. The
Swingfires went back to the RAC in 1984.

[109] Presumably, the two new battalions came along with the brigade headquarters.
Some sources have shown 5th Field Force split between Germany and Catterick, but it
appears that the units officially assigned were all in Germany.

3rd Armoured Division	Soest
TF Echo	Paderborn
TF Foxtrot	Soest
4th Armoured Division	Herford
TF Golf	Minden
TF Hotel	Detmold

In Jan 1981 the task force headquarters reverted to brigade designations, bringing back some numbers (22nd and 33rd) long gone from the Army's orbat, along with the six more recent BAOR brigade numbers. There was no change in assignments—each division had two brigades in lieu of the two task force headquarters—but division units were gradually realigned under the brigade headquarters.

The redesignations of the task forces to brigades was as follows:
> TF Alpha at Soltau became 7th Armoured Brigade
> TF Bravo at Hohne became 22nd Armoured Brigade
> TF Charlie at Munster became 4th Armoured Brigade
> TF Delta at Osnabrück became 12th Armoured Brigade
> TF Echo at Paderborn became 33^{d} Armoured Brigade
> TF Foxtrot at Soest became 6th Armoured Brigade
> TF Golf at Minden became 11th Armoured Brigade
> TF Hotel at Detmold became 20th Armoured Brigade

5th Field Force lingered until Jan 1982, when its headquarters relocated to Catterick and resumed its old designation of 24th Infantry Brigade. Most of its components appear to have gone to the divisions ca. Jan 1981, and it was reformed in the UK with new units. Its artillery regiment and engineer squadron remained for a period in Germany.

A detailed orbat for this period (Jan 1981 to Jan 1983) appears below at page 93.

As already noted, by the 1970s, the drain of security operations in Northern Ireland had a major impact on BOAR. Units of all arms (including infantry, artillery, and transport) were called for four-month roulement tours there. A unit might need two months to prepare for the tour, and time afterwards to revert to its normal role. The effect was to pull units away from Germany and their normal role for up to eight months at a time. This left vacancies in units (up to one third of a division, by one estimate) and impacted on mechanised warfare training.

Support

In 1971 1ˢᵗ Artillery Brigade still had two regiments with their M107 SP 175mm howitzers and a locating regiment for target acquisition, along with three surviving missile regiments (mixed Honest John rockets and M110 SP 8" howitzers). 39ᵗʰ Missile Regiment RA (stationed in the Paderborn/Sennelager area) left Germany in Apr 1972; it gave up its launchers in 1973, converting to 39ᵗʰ Medium Regiment RA, under which designation it would later return to BAOR. From 1976 the British began to phase out the regiments with Honest John rockets. 24ᵗʰ Missile Regiment RA was amalgamated in Feb 1977 with the surviving unit, the 50ᵗʰ. 50ᵗʰ Missile Regiment RA was converted to the Lance SSM between 1975 and ca. Sep 1977, with four batteries of three launchers each. There were various changes in the assigned gun regiments during the period.

At the beginning of this period 7ᵗʰ Artillery Brigade (AA)—headquarters now at Dortmund—had two light air defence regiments RA with 40mm Bofors guns. The 36ᵗʰ Heavy AD Regt RA (returning to BAOR in 1971 with its Thunderbird SAMs) was disbanded the end of Dec 1977;[110] the two remaining regiments had earlier converted to the new Rapier SAM.

Both 1ˢᵗ Artillery Brigade and the 7ᵗʰ Artillery Brigade (AA) were disbanded 1 Sep 1977 and their elements absorbed by the new 1ˢᵗ Artillery Division (with HQ at Dortmund). At this point, the division had a missile regiment with the Lance SSM; a heavy regiment with the M107; and the locating regiment all in the ground role. Air defence was provided by the two air defence regiments RA with Rapier SAM: note that "Light" was now gone from their titles.

In Nov 1971 9ᵗʰ Regiment AAC was formed with two squadrons as a direct subordinate to 1 Corps. Since one squadron was soon disbanded, this represented little real change from prior periods.

The engineer stores regiment was disbanded in 1977, leaving very little in the way of GHQ engineers in BAOR, although a field squadron was sent to Germany in 1973 to support the RAF's Harriers. The only RE unit directly under 1 Corps by 1977 was a corps field park squadron. A new amphibious engineer regiment was formed in 1970, taking over the existing amphibious engineer squadron and adding an additional one.

The organization and deployment of signals regiments was relatively stable during this period.

---

[110] It ceased to be operational 1 Sep 1977.

▱ *BAOR 1971–1976*

HQ BAOR   *Rheindahlen*

HQ 4th Signal Group   *Rheindahlen*
     13th Signal Regt (Radio)   *Birgelen*
     16th Signal Regt   *Krefeld*
     21st Signal Regt (Air Formation)*Lemgo*
     28th Signal Regt   *St Tonis*

40 Advanced Engr Stores Regt   *Wilich*
     21 Park Sqn RE and 41 Plant Sqn RE
10 Field Sqn RE[111] [assigned Jan 1973] *RAF Laarbruch*
14 Topographic Sqn RE   *Mönchen-Gladbach*

HQ 1 (British) Corps   *Bielefeld*
7th Signal Regt   *Herford*
22nd Signal Regt   *Lippstadt*

5th Royal Inniskilling DG [recce]   *Herford* [left May 1971]
     replaced Jun 1971 by Royal Scots DG
     replaced Oct 1972 by 14th/20th Hussars
     replaced Mar 1976 by 1st Royal Tank Regt
3rd Royal Tank Regiment [recce]   *Wolfenbüttel*
     replaced Nov 1971 by 17th/21st Lancers
     replaced Oct 1974 by 16th/5th Lancers

▣ **1st Artillery Brigade**   *Hildesheim*
24th Missile Regt RA[112]   *Paderborn*; moved Nov 1972 to *Dortmund*
     51, 76 Btys RA [HJ rockets] and 2, 34 Btys RA [M110]
39th Missile Regt RA   *Paderborn* [left Apr 1972]
     19, 36 Btys RA [HJ rockets] and H, 171 Btys RA [M110]
50th Missile Regt RA   *Menden*
     15, 21 Btys RA [HJ rockets] and 33, 56 Btys RA [M110]
20th Heavy Regt RA   *Fallingbostel*
     12, 27, 43 Hy Btys RA [M107]
     replaced Nov 1971 by 42nd Heavy Regiment RA {18, 49, 94 Hy Btys
         RA}

---

[111] Harrier support squadron.
[112] In 1972, 19th Bty RA replaced 34th Bty RA.

[1st Artillery Brigade]
32nd Heavy Regt RA   *Hildesheim*
        46, 50, 74 Btys RA [M107]
        replaced Nov 1972 by 5th Heavy Regiment RA {K, P, Q Hy Btys RA}
94th Locating Regt RA   *Celle*
        57, 73, 156 Loc Btys RA
3rd Carabiniers[113]   *Munster*
        replaced May 1971 by 2nd Bn Royal Anglian Regt
        replaced May 1976 by 1st Bn Royal Scots
218th Signal Sqn   *Hildesheim*

□ **7th Artillery Brigade (AA)**   *Dortmund*
36th HyAD Regt RA   [arrived Nov 1971] *Dortmund* [disbanded Nov 1977]
        10, 111 AD Btys RA [Thunderbird]
16th LtAD Regt RA   *Soest* [left Dec 1977]
        14, 30, 32 LtAD Btys RA [40mm Bofors]
12th LtAD Regt RA   *Dortmund*
        T, 9, 58 LtAD Btys RA [40mm]
        replaced 1972 by 22nd LtAD Regt RA {11, 42, 53 LtAD Btys RA}[114]
        replaced Sep 1975 by 12th LtAD Regt RA [Rapier]}
217th Signal Sqn   *Hildesheim*

28 Amphibious Engineer Regt   *Hameln*
        23, 64 Amphib Sqns, 73 Field Sqn, 71 HQ Sqn RE
65 Corps Support Sqn RE   *Osnabrück*

1st Wing Army Air Corps   *Detmold*[115]
        669th Sqn AAC [formed Jun 1971]   *Wildenrath*
9th Regt AAC [formed Nov 1971]   *Detmold*
        655th Sqn AAC   *Detmold*[116]
        669th Sqn AAC [u/c Nov-Dec 1971 only]   *Detmold*

---

[113] Served as nuclear escort battalion. 8th Regiment RCT was actually responsible for transport and safe custody of tactical nuclear warheads.
[114] 40mm Bofors; converted to Rapier SAM 1973.
[115] Existence of this headquarters into 1971 unclear, although it apparently lingered as 669th Sqn AAC has been shown as assigned to it when the squadron was formed in Germany. It more likely had become HQ Army Aviation, BAOR. 669th Sqn AAC returned to it in Jan 1972.
[116] An independent squadron formed 1969 from 18th Flight AAC for duty with 1 Corps. Transferred to new 9th Regiment AAC in Nov 1971. The squadron was disbanded in 1976, but RHQ 9th Regiment AAC lingered on.

1 Corps RCT   *locations unknown*
      7 Tank Transporter Regt
      10 Regt RCT
      21 Sqn RCT

1 Corps Combat Supplies Bn RAOC   *Paderborn*
7 Guided Missile Coy RAOC   *Wulfen*
56 (Special Weapons) Bty RA   *location unknown*
5 (Special Weapons) Sqn RCT   *location unknown*
8 Artillery Support Regt RCT   *location unknown*

1 Corps Troops Ordnance Field Park *location unknown*
1 (Corps) Field Workshop REME   *Bielefeld*
1 Corps RAMC   *location unknown*

▭ 1st Division

1st Division HQ & Signal Regt   *Verden*
4th Field Regt RA   *Munsterlager*
      29, 88, 97 Field Btys RA [Abbot]
      replaced Feb 1974 by 25th Field Regt RA {35, 54, 93 Field Btys RA}
          at *Paderborn*
26th Field Regt RA   *Hohne*
      16, 17, 159 Field Btys RA [Abbot]
      replaced Aug 1971 by 49th Field Regt RA {55, 127, 143 Fd Btys RA}
45th Medium Regt RA   *Paderborn*
      18, 52, 170, 176 Mdm Btys RA[117] [M109]
1st Division RE   *Nienburg*
      21 Engineer Regt   *Nienburg*
         1, 4 Field Sqns RE
      32 Armoured Engineer Regt[118] *Hohne*
         30, 37 Field Sqns RE
      26 Armoured Engineer Sqn RE *Hohne*
      45 Field Sp Sqn RE   *Nienburg*
1st Regt AAC   *Hildesheim*
      651st Sqn AAC   *Verden*
      657th Sqn AAC   *Minden*
      658th Sqn AAC   *Soltau*
1st Division Transport Regt RCT {12, 66 Sqns} *Bunde?*

---

[117] In Nov 1972 34th Mdm Bty RA replaced 176th Mdm Bty RA.
[118] Although allowed to retain its traditional name, 32 was now a normal engineer field regiment.

[1st Division]
1st Division RAOC   *location unknown*
1st Division REME {7 & 11 Workshops}   *location unknown*
1st Division RAMC   *location unknown*

▢ 7th ARMOURED BRIGADE
HQ and 207th Signal Sqn   *Soltau*
Queens Own Hussars   *Hohne*
       replaced Jul 1974 by 13th/18th Hussars
4th Royal Tank Regt   *Hohne*
       replaced Jan 1973 by 1st Queens Dragoon Guards
1st Bn Green Howards   *Minden* [left Jan 1974]
       replaced Nov 1974 by 1st Bn KOR Border Regt
1st Bn Royal Green Jackets   *Celle*
       replaced Apr 1974 by 1st Bn POWO Regt of Yorkshire

▢ 11TH ARMOURED BRIGADE
HQ and 211th Signal Sqn   *Minden*
15th/19th Hussars   *Fallingbostel*
       replaced Nov 1974 by 17th/21st Lancers
16th/5th Lancers   *Fallingbostel*
       replaced Nov 1971 by 3rd Royal Tank Regt
       replaced Oct 1976 by 14th/20th Hussars
1st Bn King's Regt   *Minden*
       replaced Nov 1971 by 3rd Bn Light Infantry
       replaced Jun 1976 by 1st Bn Duke of Wellington's Regt
1st Bn Gloucestershire Regt [assigned Jan 1971]   *Minden*
       replaced May 1975 by 1st Bn Cheshire Regt

▢ **2nd Division**[119]
2nd Division HQ & Signal Regt   *Lubbecke*
2nd Field Regt RA [assigned Jan 1971]   *Hemer*
       L, N, O Field Btys RA [Abbot]
40th Field Regt RA   *Gütersloh*
       38, 129, 137 Field Btys RA [Abbot]

---

[119] 2nd Division began experimenting with a new organization Sep 1976.

[2nd Division]
39th Medium Regt RA [assigned Nov 1972]   *Paderborn*
   H, 132, 176 Btys [M109]
2nd Division RE   *Lubbecke*
  23 Engineer Regt   *Lubbecke*
   7, 16 Field Sqns RE
  25 Engineer Regt   *Osnabrück*
   12, 39 Field Sqns RE
  31 Armoured Engineer Sqn RE   *Osnabrück*
  43 Field Sp Sqn RE   *Lubbecke?*
2nd Regt AAC   *Munster*
  652nd Sqn AAC   *Bunde*
  659th Sqn AAC   *Detmold*
  660th Sqn AAC   *Munster*
2nd Division Transport Regt {4, 33 Sqns}   Bunde
2nd Division RAOC   *location unknown*
2nd Division REME {4 & 12 Workshops}   *location unknown*
2nd Division RAMC   *location unknown*

4th ARMOURED BRIGADE
HQ and 204th Signal Sqn   *Munster*
5th Royal Inniskilling DG   *Munster*
  replaced Nov 1974 by 4th Royal Tank Regt
13th/18th Hussars   *Munster*
  replaced Aug 1972 by 2nd Royal Tank Regt
2nd Bn Coldstream Guards   *Munster*
  replaced Feb 1972 by 1st Bn Grenadier Gds
  replaced Jan 1975 by 1st Bn Irish Gds
1st Bn Welsh Guards   *Munster*
  replaced Sep 1972 by 1st Bn Scots Gds
  replaced Jan 1976 by 2nd Bn Scots Gds

12TH MECHANISED BRIGADE
HQ and 212th Signal Sqn   *Osnabrück*
1st Royal Tank Regt   *Osnabrück*
  replaced May 1973 by Royal Scots Dgn Gds
  replaced Dec 1976 by 5th Royal Inniskilling Dgn Gds
1st Bn Royal Regt of Wales   *Osnabrück*
  replaced Jul 1973 by 1st Bn Staffordshire Regt

[12th Mechanised Brigade]
1st Bn Queens Lancashire Regt   *Osnabrück*
       replaced Jan 1975 by 1st Bn Argyll & Sutherland Highlanders
1st Bn Queens Own Highlanders [assigned Apr 1971]   *Osnabrück*
       replaced Jun 1976 by 1st Bn Devonshire & Dorset Regt

☐ **4th Division**
4th Division HQ & Signal Regt   *Herford*
1st Field Regt RHA   *Detmold*
     A, B, E Btys RHA [Abbot]
19th Field Regt RA [assigned Mar 1971]   *Dortmund*
     25, 28, 67 Field Btys RA [Abbot]
     replaced Aug 1974 by 26th Medium Regt RA {16, 17, 159 Btys RA
        [M109]}
27th Medium Regt RA   *Lippstadt*
     6, 23, 132 Btys RA [M109]
4th Division RE   *Iserlohn*
     26 Engineer Regt   *Iserlohn*
       5, 25 Field Sqns RE
     35 Engineer Regt   *Hameln*
       29, 42 Field Sqns RE
     2 Armoured Engineer Sqn RE   *Iserlohn*
     44 Field Sp Sqn RE   *Iserlohn*
4th Regt AAC   *Detmold*
     654th Sqn AAC   *Minden*
     661st Sqn AAC   *Herford*
     662nd Sqn AAC   *Minden*
4th Division Transport Regt { 11, 15 Sqns}   *Minden*
4th Division RAOC   *location unknown*
4th Division REME {6 & 20 Workshops}   *location unknown*
4th Division RAMC   *location unknown*

☐ **6th ARMOURED BRIGADE**[120]
HQ and 206th Signal Sqn   *Soest*
Queens Royal Irish Hussars [assigned Aug 1970]   *Paderborn*
4th/7th Dragoon Guards [assigned Sep 1970]   *Sennelager*
     replaced Jun 1973 by Royal Hussars

---

[120] Brigade HQ (then 6th Infantry Brigade) had gone to the UK in 1968, leaving the assigned armoured regiments in Germany. It returned in 1971.

[6th Armoured Brigade]
2nd Bn Queens Regt [assigned Dec 1970]   *Werl*
          replaced Sep 1975 by 1st Bn Queens Regt
1st Bn Royal Irish Rangers [assigned Sep 1970]   *Hemer*
          replaced Jul 1974 by 2nd Bn Royal Irish Rangers

20TH ARMOURED BRIGADE
HQ and 200th Signal Sqn   *Detmold*
Blues & Royals   *Detmold*
          replaced Sep 1971 by Life Guards
          replaced Oct 1975 by Blues & Royals
1st Queens Dragoon Guards   *Detmold*
          replaced Jan 1971 by 9th/12th Lancers
          replaced May 1976 by Queen's Own Hussars
3rd Bn Royal Anglian Regt   *Paderborn*
          replaced Aug 1975 by 2nd Bn Royal Regt of Fusiliers
1st Bn Light Infantry   *Lemgo*
          replaced Mar 1974 by 2nd Bn Light Infantry

▱ *BAOR 1977—1980*[121]

HQ BAOR   *Rheindahlen*

HQ 4th Signal Group   *Rheindahlen*
      13th Signal Regt (Radio)   *Birgelen*
      16th Signal Regt   *Krefeld*
      21st Signal Regt (Air Formation)   *Lemgo*
      28th Signal Regt   *St Tonis*
      14th (EW) Signal Regt [formed 1977]   *Celle*

40 Advanced Engr Stores Regt   *Wilich* [disbanded Oct 1977][122]
      21 Park Sqn RE and 41 Plant Sqn RE
10 Field Sqn RE [Harrier Force support]   *RAF Laarbruch*
14 Topographic Sqn RE   *Mönchen-Gladbach*

1 (British) Corps   *Bielefeld*
7th Signal Regt   *Herford*
22nd Signal Regt   *Lippstadt*

▱ **1st Artillery Division**   *Dortmund*
50th Missile Regt RA   *Menden*
      15, 19, 36, 51 Btys RA [Lance SSM]
5th Heavy Regt RA   *Hildesheim*
      K, P, Q Btys RA [M107]; 18 Bty RA [M110]
94th Locating Regt RA   *Celle*
      57, 73, 156 Loc Btys RA
12th Air Defence Regt RA   *Dortmund*
      T, 9, 58 AD Btys RA [Rapier SAM]
      replaced May 1981 by 16th AD Regt RA {14, 30, 32 AD Btys RA}
22nd Air Defence Regt RA [assigned Dec 1977]   *Dortmund*
      11, 42, 53 AD Btys RA [Rapier SAM]
1st Bn Royal Scots [nuclear escort battalion]   *Munster*
      relieved Apr 1979 by 1st Bn Gloucestershire Regt
8th Artillery Support Regt RCT   *Munster*

28 Amphibious Engineer Regt   *Hameln*
      23, 64 Amphib Sqns and 71 HQ Sqn RE
65 Corps Sp Sqn RE   *Osnabrück*

---

[121] The reorganization to the new structure occurred Mar-Dec 1977.
[122] 21 Park Sqn RE survived as an independent unit, becoming 21 Sp Sqn RE.

32 Armoured Engineer Regt [reformed 1980]   *Verden*
  26 and 31 Armd Engr Sqns[123]

9th Regt AAC   *Detmold*
  659th Sqn AAC   *Detmold*
  669th Sqn AAC   *Detmold*

7th Tank Transporter Regt RCT *Sennelager*
10th Regt RCT *Bielefeld*
21st Sqn RCT *location unknown*
1 Corps Combat Supplies Bn RAOC *Paderborn*
1 (Corps) Field Workshop REME *Bielefeld*
1 Corps RAMC *location unknown*

1st ARMOURED DIVISION

1st Armoured Division HQ & Signal Regt *Verden*
Task Force Alpha, HQ and 207 Signal Sqn *Soltau*
Task Force Bravo, HQ & 201 Signal Sqn *Hohne*
1st Queens Dragoon Gds[recce] *Hohne*
  replaced Nov 1980 by 9th/12th Lancers
4th/7th Dragoon Gds *Minden*
14th/20th Hussars *Hohne*
17th/21st Lancers *Fallingbostel*
  replaced Dec 1977 by 1st Bn Coldstream Guards
  replaced Dec 1980 by 2nd Bn Coldstream Guards
1st Bn POWO Regt of Yorkshire *Celle*
  replaced Aug 1978 by 1st Bn Royal Anglian Regt
3rd Bn Royal Regt of Fusiliers *Fallingbostel*
45th Field Regt RA *Hohne*
  52, 170 Btys RA [M109], 34 Bty RA [M110]
49th Field Regt RA *Hohne*
  55, 94, 127, 143 Btys RA [Abbott]
10th AD Bty RA [Blowpipe] *location unknown*
D Bty RHA [Swingfire ATGW] *Hohne*
1st Armoured Division RE *Nienburg*
  1, 4, 7 Field Sqns and 45 Field Sp Sqn RE
1st Regt AAC *Hildesheim*
  651, 661 Sqns AAC

[123] 26 Armd Engr Sqn RE reformed Apr 1978 at Munsterlager, and joined the new regiment in 1980; 31 Armd Engr Sqn RE formed 1980 with the regiment.

[1st Armoured Division]
1st Armoured Division Transport Regt {12, 66 Sqns}   *location unknown*
1st Armoured Division RAOC – 1 Ordnance Coy   *location unknown*
1st Armoured Division REME – 7 Workshop   *Fallingbostel*
1st Armoured Division RAMC – Field Ambulance   *location unknown*

2nd ARMOURED DIVISION

2nd Armoured Division HQ & Signal Regt   *Lubbecke*
Task Force Charlie, HQ and 204 Signal Sqn   *Munster*
Task Force Delta, HQ & 212 Signal Sqn   *Osnabrück*
1st Royal Tank Regt [recce]   *Hohne*
5th Royal Inniskilling Dgn Gds   *Osnabrück*
4th Royal Tank Regt   *Munster*
2nd Bn Scots Guards   *Munster*
        replaced Feb 1978 by 2nd Bn Grenadier Guards
1st Bn Devonshire & Dorset Regt   *Osnabrück*
        replaced Apr 1980 by 1st Bn King's Regt
1st Bn Argyll & Sutherland Highlanders   *Osnabrück*
        replaced Aug 1978 by 1st Bn Duke of Edinburgh's Royal Regt
27th Field Regt RA   *Lippstadt*
        6, 56 Btys RA [M109], 23 Bty RA [M110]
40th Field Regt RA   *Gütersloh*
        38, 49, 129 137 Btys RA [Abbot]
        replaced Mar 1981 by 47th Field Regt RA {3, 4, 31, 49 Btys RA}
21st AD Bty RA [Blowpipe]   *location unknown*
C Bty RHA [Swingfire ATGW]   *Gütersloh*
2nd Armoured Division RE   *Lubbecke*
        12, 16, 39 Field Sqns, 43 Field Sp Sqn RA
2nd Regt AAC   *Munster*
        652, 662 Sqns
2nd Armoured Division Transport Regt {4, 33 Sqns}   *Bunde*
2nd Armoured Division RAOC – 2 Ordnance Coy   *location unknown*
2nd Armoured Division REME – 12 Workshop   *Osnabrück*
2nd Armoured Division RAMC – Field Ambulance   *location unknown*

▣ **3ʳᴰ Armoured Division**

3ʳᵈ Armoured Division HQ & Signal Regt   *Soest*
Task Force Echo, HQ and 202 Signal Sqn   *Paderborn*
Task Force Foxtrot, HQ and 206 Signal Sqn   *Soest*
Queen's Royal Irish Hussars [recce]   *Paderborn*
            replaced Jan 1978 by 3ʳᵈ Royal Tank Regt
Royal Hussars   *Sennelager*
            replaced Apr 1979 by Royal Scots Dragoon Guards
15ᵗʰ/19ᵗʰ Hussars [assigned Jan 1978]   *Paderborn*
1ˢᵗ Bn Queen's Regt   *Werl*
            replaced Apr 1980 by 1ˢᵗ Bn Black Watch
2ⁿᵈ Bn Royal Regt of Fusiliers   *Paderborn*; Oct 1977 to *Hemer*
            replaced Oct 1979 by 1ˢᵗ Bn Worcestershire & Sherwood Foresters
2ⁿᵈ Bn Royal Irish Rangers   *Hemer*
            replaced Mar 1979 by 1ˢᵗ Bn Royal Highland Fusiliers
2ⁿᵈ Field Regt RA   *Dortmund*
            L, N, O Btys RA [Abbott]
            replaced Aug 197 9 by 19ᵗʰ Field Regt RA {5, 13, 25, 28 Btys RA}
26th Field Regt RA   *Dortmund*
            16, 17 Btys RA [M109], 76 Bty RA [M110]
111ᵗʰ AD Bty RA [Blowpipe]   *Dortmund*
M Bty RHA [Swingfire ATGW]   *Dortmund*
3ʳᵈ Armoured Division RE   *Iserlohn*
            5, 25, 30 Field Sqns, 2 Field Sp Sqn RE
3ʳᵈ Regt AAC   *Soest*
            653, 663 Sqns
3ʳᵈ Armoured Division Transport Regt {1, 7 Sqns ?}   *location unknown*
3ʳᵈ Armoured Division RAOC – 3 Ordnance Coy   *location unknown*
3ʳᵈ Armoured Division REME – 5 Workshop   *Soest*
3ʳᵈ Armoured Division RAMC – Field Ambulance   *location unknown*

▣ **4ᵗʰ Armoured Division**

4ᵗʰ Armoured Division HQ & Signal Regt   *Herford*
Task Force Golf, HQ & 211 Signal Sqn   *Minden*
Task Force Hotel, HQ & 200 Signal Sqn   *Detmold*
16ᵗʰ/5ᵗʰ Lancers [recce]   *Wolfenbüttel*
            replaced Jan 1981 by 2ⁿᵈ Royal Tank Regt
Blues and Royals   *Detmold*
            replaced Feb 1980 by Life Guards
Queens Own Hussars   *Detmold*

[4th Armoured Division]
1st Bn Cheshire Regt   *Minden*
        replaced Aug 1977 by 1st Bn Royal Regt of Fusiliers
1st Bn Duke of Wellington's Regt   *Minden*
        replaced Nov 1980 by 2nd Bn Royal Green Jackets
2nd Bn Light Infantry   *Lemgo*
        replaced Jan 1978 by 1st Bn Royal Welch Fusiliers
25th Field Regt RA   *Munsterlager*; Jan 1978 to :*Paderborn*
        5, 35, 54, 93 Btys RA [Abbot]
39th Field Regt RA   *Paderborn*
        132, 176 Btys RA [M109], H Bty RA [M110]
43rd AD Bty RA [Blowpipe]   *Paderborn*
J Bty RHA [Swingfire ATGW]   *Paderborn*
4th Armoured Division RE   *Hameln*
        29, 37, 42 Field Sqns; 44 Field Sp Sqn RE
4th Regt AAC   *Detmold*
        654, 664 Sqns
4th Armoured Division Transport Regt {11, 15 Sqns}   *location unknown*
4th Armoured Division RAOC – 4 Ordnance Coy   *location unknown*
4th Armoured Division REME – 4 Workshop   *Detmold*
4th Armoured Division RAMC – Field Ambulance   *location unknown*

⊠ **5th Field Force**
HQ & 210 Signal Sqn   *Osnabrück*
2nd Royal Tank Regt [recce]   *Munster*
        replaced May 1979 by 9th/12th Lancers
        replaced Nov 1980 by 17th/21st Lancers
1st Bn Devonshire & Dorset Regt   *Osnabrück*
1st Bn Irish Gds   *Munster*
        replaced Nov 1977 by 1st Bn Royal Hampshire Regt
3rd Bn Parachute Regt [assigned Mar 1977]   *Osnabrück*
        replaced Jun 1980 by 1st Bn KO Scottish Borderers
7th Regt RHA   *Osnabrück*
        F, G, I Btys RHA [FH70]
73 Field Sqn RE   *Osnabrück*
655 Sqn AAC   UK (*Topcliffe*)
Tpt Sqn RCT   *Osnabrück?*
5 Ordnance Coy   *Osnabrück*
15 Workshop REME   *Osnabrück*
Field Ambulance   *Osnabrück*

◻ *BAOR Jan 1981—Jan 1983*

HQ BAOR   *Rheindahlen*

HQ 4th Signal Group   *Rheindahlen*
    13th Signal Regt (Radio)   *Birgelen*
    14th (EW) Signal Regt   *Celle*
    16th Signal Regt   *Krefeld*
    21st Signal Regt (Air Formation)   *Lemgo*
    28th Signal Regt   *St Tonis*

10 Field Sqn RE [Harrier Force support]   *RAF Laarbruch*
14 Topographic Sqn RE   *Mönchen-Gladbach*

1 (British) Corps   *Bielefeld*
664 Sqn AAC   *Detmold*
7th Signal Regt   *Herford*
22nd Signal Regt   *Lippstadt*

◻ **Artillery Division** *Dortmund*
50th Missile Regt RA   *Menden*
    15, 19, 36, 51 Btys RA [Lance SSM]
5th Heavy Regt RA   *Hildesheim*
    K, P, 18 Btys RA [M110]; Q Loc Bty RA
39th Heavy Regt RA   *Sennelager*
    34, 56, 76 Hy Btys RA [M107]
32nd Heavy Regt RA [arrived Apr 1982]   *Dortmund*
    12, 25, 27, 46 Hy Btys RA [M107]
94th Locating Regt RA   *Celle*
    57, 73, 156 Loc Btys RA
12th Air Defense Regt RA   *Dortmund*
    T, 9, 58 AD Btys RA [Rapier SAM]
    replaced May 1981 by 16th Air Def Regt RA {14, 30, 32 AD Btys RA}
22nd Air Defense Regt RA   *Dortmund*
    11, 42, 53 AD Btys RA [Rapier SAM]
1st Bn Gloucestershire Regt [nuclear escort battalion]   *Munster* [left Oct
        1981 w/o replacement]
8th Artillery Support Regt RCT[124]   *Munster*

---

[124] In 1981 the regiment incorporated 10 platoons of pioneers and RCT soldiers in the infantry role, replacing the former infantry escort battalion.

28 Amphibious Engineer Regt   *Hameln*
        23, 64 Amphib Sqns and 71 HQ Sqn RE
32 Armoured Engineer Regt   *Verden*
        26, 31, 77 Armd Engr Sqns
65 Corps Sp Sqn RE   *Osnabrück*

9th Regt AAC   *Detmold* [disbanded Dec 1982]
        659th Sqn AAC   *Detmold*
        669th Sqn AAC   *Detmold*

7th Tank Transporter Regt RCT   *Sennelager*
10th Regt RCT   *Bielefeld*
21st Sqn RCT   *location unknown*
1 Corps Combat Supplies Bn RAOC   *Paderborn*
1 (Corps) Field Workshop REME   *Bielefeld*
1 Corps RAMC   *location unknown*

1st ARMOURED DIVISION
1st Armoured Division HQ & Signal Regt   *Verden*
9th/12th Lancers [recce]   *Hohne*
        replaced Nov 1982 by 1st Queen's Dragoon Guards
7th Armoured Brigade HQ and 207 Signal Sqn   *Soltau*
        4th/7th Dragoon Gds   *Minden*
                replaced Apr 1981 by Royal Hussars at *Soltau*
        14th/20th Hussars   *Hohne*
        3rd Bn Royal Regt of Fusiliers   *Fallingbostel*
                replaced Mar 1981 by 3rd Bn Queen's Regt
22nd Armoured Brigade HQ & 201 Signal Sqn   *Hohne*
        2nd Bn Coldstream Guards   *Fallingbostel*
                replaced Nov 1982 by 2nd Royal Tank Regt
        1st Bn Irish Guards   *Munster*
                replaced Aug 1978 by 3rd Bn Royal Regt of Fusiliers
        1st Bn Royal Anglian Regt   *Celle*
                replaced Apr 1982 by 3rd Bn Royal Green Jackets
45th Field Regt RA   *Hohne*
        34, 52, 170 Btys RA [M109],
49th Field Regt RA   *Hohne*
        55, 127, 143 Btys RA [Abbott]
        replaced Apr 1982 by 1st Regt RHA {A, B, E Btys RHA}
21st AD Bty RA [Blowpipe]   *Lippstadt*
D Bty RHA [Swingfire ATGW]   *Hohne*

[1st Armoured Division]
21 Engineer Regt   *Nienburg*
          1, 4, 7 Field Sqns and 45 Field Sp Sqn RE
1st Regt AAC   *Hildesheim*
          651, 661 Sqns AAC
1st Armoured Division Transport Regt {12, 66 Sqns}   *location unknown*
1st Armoured Division RAOC – 1 Ordnance Coy   *location unknown*
1st Armoured Division REME – 7 Workshop   *Fallingbostel*
1st Armoured Division RAMC – Field Ambulance   *location unknown*

⊡ 2nd ARMOURED DIVISION[125]
2nd Armoured Division HQ & Signal Regt   *Lubbecke*
1st Royal Tank Regt [recce]   *Hohne*
4th Armoured Brigade HQ and 204 Signal Sqn   *Munster*
          5th Royal Inniskilling Dgn Gds   *Osnabrück*
          4th Royal Tank Regt   *Munster*
                    replaced Jul 1982 by Queen's Royal Irish Hussars
          2nd Bn Grenadier Guards   *Munster*
                    replaced Aug 1981 by 1st Bn Irish Guards
12th Armoured Brigade HQ & 212 Signal Sqn   *Osnabrück*
          17th/21st Lancers   *Munster*
          1st Bn King's Regt   *Osnabrück*
          1st Bn Duke of Edinburgh's Royal Regt   *Osnabrück*
          1st Bn KO Scottish Borders [assigned Jan 1982]   *Osnabrück*
27th Field Regt RA   *Lippstadt*
          6, 23, 56 Btys RA [M109]
40th Field Regt RA   *Gütersloh*
          38, 49, 129 137 Btys RA [Abbot]
          replaced Mar 1981 by 47th Field Regt RA {3, 4, 31, 49 Btys RA}
10th AD Bty RA [Blowpipe]   *Gütersloh*
C Bty RHA [Swingfire ATGW]   *Gütersloh*
23 Engineer Regt   *Lubbecke*
          12, 16, 39 Field Sqns, 43 Field Sp Sqn RA
2nd Regt AAC   *Munster*
          652, 662 Sqns
2nd Armoured Division Transport Regt {4, 33 Sqns}   *Bunde*
2nd Armoured Division RAOC – 2 Ordnance Coy   *location unknown*
2nd Armoured Division REME – 12 Workshop   *Osnabrück*
2nd Armoured Division RAMC – Field Ambulance   *location unknown*

---

[125] 2nd Armoured Division closed down in Germany ca. Dec 1982 and reopened in York as 2nd Infantry Division Jan 1983.

▱ **3RD ARMOURED DIVISION**

3rd Armoured Division HQ & Signal Regt   *Soest*

15th/19th Hussars [recce]   *Paderborn* [left Dec 1982]

6th Armoured Brigade HQ and 206 Signal Sqn   *Soest*[126]

        1st Bn Worcestershire & Sherwood Foresters   *Hemer*

        1st Bn Light Infantry [arrived Mar 1981]   *Hemer*

33rd Armoured Brigade HQ and 202 Signal Sqn *Paderborn*

        Royal Scots Dragoon Guards   *Sennelager*

        1st Bn Royal Highland Fusiliers   *Paderborn*

        1st Bn Black Watch   *Werl*

19th Field Regt RA   *Dortmund*

     5, 13, 25, 28 Btys RA [Abbott]

26th Field Regt RA   *Dortmund*

     16, 17, 76 Btys RA [M109]

111th AD Bty RA [Blowpipe]   *Dortmund*

M Bty RHA [Swingfire ATGW]   *Dortmund*

26 Engineer Regt   *Iserlohn*

     5, 25, 30 Field Sqns, 2 Field Sp Sqn RE

3rd Regt AAC   *Soest*

     653, 663 Sqns

3rd Armoured Division Transport Regt {1, 7 Sqns ?}   *location unknown*

3rd Armoured Division RAOC – 3 Ordnance Coy   *location unknown*

3rd Armoured Division REME – 5 Workshop   *Soest*

3rd Armoured Division RAMC – Field Ambulance   *location unknown*

▱ **4th ARMOURED DIVISION**

4th Armoured Division HQ & Signal Regt   *Herford*

2nd Royal Tank Regt [recce]   *Wolfenbüttel*

     replaced Nov 1982 by 15th/19th Hussars at *Paderborn*

11th Armoured Brigade HQ & 211 Signal Sqn   *Minden*

        3rd Royal Tank Regt   *Munster*

        1st Bn Royal Regt of Fusiliers   *Minden*

        2nd Bn Royal Green Jackets   *Minden*

20th Armoured Brigade HQ & 200 Signal Sqn   *Detmold*

        Life Guards   *Detmold*

        Queens Own Hussars   *Detmold*

            replaced Jan 1983 by 4th/7th Dragoon Gds

        1st Bn Royal Welch Fusiliers   *Lemgo*

            replaced Aug 1982 by 1st Bn Royal Regt of Wales

---

[126] The assigned tank regiment, if any, is unknown.

[4th Armoured Division]
25th Field Regt RA   *Paderborn*
          5, 35, 54, 93 Btys RA [Abbot]
39th Field Regt RA   *Paderborn*
          132, 176 Btys RA [M109], H Bty RA [M110]
          replaced Apr 1982 by 2nd Field Regt RA {L, N, O Btys RA [M109]
                    at *Dortmund*
43rd AD Bty RA [Blowpipe]   *Paderborn*
J Bty RHA [Swingfire ATGW]   *Paderborn*
35th Engineer Regt   *Hameln*
          29, 37, 42 Field Sqns; 44 Field Sp Sqn RE
4th Regt AAC   *Detmold*
          654, 664 Sqns
4th Armoured Division Transport Regt {11, 15 Sqns}   *location unknown*
4th Armoured Division RAOC – 4 Ordnance Coy   *location unknown*
4th Armoured Division REME – 4 Workshop   *Detmold*
4th Armoured Division RAMC – Field Ambulance   *location unknown*

⊠ **5th Field Force**
HQ & 210 Signal Sqn   *Osnabrück* [left Jan 1982][127]
1st Bn KO Scottish Borderers   *Osnabrück* [left Jan 1982]
7th Regt RHA (F, G, I Btys RHA) [FH70] remained at Osnabrück to Apr 1984,
          intended for 24th Infantry Brigade when it deployed to Germany
73rd Field Sqn RE also remained at Osnabrück to the end of 1982, intended for
          24th Infantry Brigade when it deployed to Germany

⊠ **24th Infantry Brigade**[128]
HQ and 210 Signal Squadron
1st Bn Green Howards
          replaced Jan 1983 by 2nd Bn Royal Regiment of Fusiliers
1st Bn Duke of Wellington's Regiment
2nd Bn Light Infantry [at Weeton]

---

[127] 5th Field Force dissolved Jan 1982; HQ reformed in the UK as HQ 24th Infantry Brigade. It appears that most of its components went to the divisions in Jan 1981.
[128] 5th Field Force redesignated 24th Infantry Brigade and relocated to Catterick Jan 1982.

The 1980s to the End

The period from 1983 probably represented the high point for BAOR in terms of professionalism and modern equipment. It also includes the only time units from Germany would go into combat, although it would be in a war far from the North German plain. And in the end, only three years after the war with Iraq, BAOR itself and most of its formations would disappear.

Formations

The new (1981) organization in BAOR did not last long, with yet another major overhaul the beginning of 1983. 2nd Armoured Division resumed its old title of 2nd Infantry Division and relocated its headquarters to York in Jan 1983. 1st, 3rd and 4th Armoured Divisions remained in Germany, with the armoured brigades partly reshuffled. 7th and 22nd Armoured Brigades remained with 1st Armoured Division, which also picked up 12th Armoured Brigade from the former 2nd Armoured Division. 4th Armoured Division kept its 11th and 20th Armoured Brigades, and picked up 33rd Armoured Brigade from the 3rd Armoured Division. That division kept its 6th Armoured Brigade and gained 4th Armoured Brigade from the former 2nd Armoured Division. To give each of the divisions in Germany three brigades, 19th Infantry Brigade (at Colchester, UK) was assigned to 3rd Armoured Division. 24th Infantry Brigade, reformed in the UK, was assigned to 2nd Infantry Division. That division also picked up two other infantry brigades in the UK (15th and 49th), and had a wartime role of returning to BAOR.[129]

As of 1 Apr 1986 the 33rd Armoured and 19th Infantry Brigades were switched between the 3rd and 4th Armoured Divisions. The Apr 1986 deployment, then, was:

1st Armoured Division	Verden
7th Armoured Brigade	Soltau
12th Armoured Brigade	Osnabrück
22nd Armoured Brigade	Hohne
3rd Armoured Division	Soest
4th Armoured Brigade	Munster
6th Armoured Brigade	Soest
33rd Armoured Brigade	Paderborn

[129] The 15th and 49th Infantry Brigades were newly-formed and consisted solely of Territorial Army units, with Regular commanders.

4th Armoured Division	Herford
11th Armoured Brigade	Minden
20th Armoured Brigade	Detmold
19th Infantry Brigade	Colchester, UK

The final orders of battle for BAOR begin below, on page 103 [1983—1990] and page 113 [1990—1994].

While the divisional brigades in Germany were all designated "armoured" they were not all organized the same. Some had two armoured regiments and one mechanised infantry battalion and the remainder one armoured regiment and two mechanised infantry battalions. Each division retained its armoured recce regiment. Artillery generally consisted of three regiments with either the 105mm Abbot or the 155mm M109.[130] The engineer field regiment remained, as did a regiment AAC.[131] The plan was to fight with two armoured divisions up and one in reserve, with 2nd Infantry Division returning to the continent for rear area security.

In 1983 6th Armoured Brigade temporarily became 6th Airmobile Brigade to test the airmobile concept in the British Army[132]. The success of these tests, in Exercise LIONHEART, led to conversion of 24th Infantry Brigade in the UK (still with a BAOR reinforcement role) to 24th Airmobile Brigade in 1988.

New types of equipment began to appear in the 1980s. From 1983, tank regiments in BAOR began trading in their Chieftains for Challenger 1. In 1983-84 7th Armoured Brigade (two regiments) was converted. In 1985-86 the two regiments in 4th Armoured Brigade converted. In 1987-88 the two regiments of 20th Armoured Brigade converted. In 1989, the single regiment in 22nd Armoured Brigade converted to Chieftain 1. Each regiment had four squadrons which meant that a total of 28 squadrons were formed. The other five BAOR tank regiments retained their Chieftains until 1992-93 (and the two UK-based regiments did so until 1993-94). In the infantry, the FV432 was gradually supplanted by a new infantry fighting vehicle, the Warrior. 1st Bn Grenadier Guards, beginning a BAOR tour in 1986, were the first battalion to convert to Warriors.

---

[130] 1st Armoured Division had two with M109 and one with Abbott, 4th Armoured Division had the reverse mix, and 3rd Armoured Division only one of each (its third regiment then being in the UK with 19th Infantry Brigade.)
[131] These varied, with either 12 Lynx AH and 6 Gazelle, or 6 Lynx AH and 12 Gazelle.
[132] Principal units were 1st Bn Gordon Highlanders and 1st Bn The Light Infantry, along with a field regiment RA, field squadron RE, and squadron AAC. The brigade, as 6th Airmobile Brigade, was without an armoured regiment. Transport helicopters to support airmobile operations belonged to the RAF, not to the Army.

Support

1st Artillery Division was redesignated 1981 simply as [the] Artillery Division (headquarters still at Dortmund). In 1984 it was redesignated as Artillery 1 (BR) Corps. 1st Artillery Brigade was reformed 1 Nov 1985 to control ground units. 50th Missile Regiment RA was reorganized Aug 1985 into three batteries; each had four Lance SSM launchers. The regiment remained in BAOR with the Lance until it was inactivated in Mar 1993. Tubed artillery included a regiment with the M110A2 (8" SP howitzer) and two depth fire regiments with the M107 (175mm SP gun). The first depth fire regiment was re-equipped with MLRS in Sep 1990 and the second one during 1991. The final regiment gave up its 8" howitzers in 1992, also converting to the MLRS. The locating regiment relocated in Jan 1985 to Larkhill in the UK.

Air defence was provided by two air defence regiments RA with the Rapier SAM (a mixture of towed and SP tracked variants). The Army had three of these regiments, allowing for some rotation between Germany and the UK.

There were no major changes to the various support units in Germany during this period.

The Gulf War

The Iraqi invasion of Kuwait in 1990 led Britain to commit forces to the Gulf. The 7th Armoured Brigade shipped from Bremerhaven, arriving in Saudi Arabia in Sep 1990. This was followed by 4th Armoured Brigade in Nov 1990, the two forming 1st (UK) Armoured Division. The two brigades had a total of three armoured regiments and three armoured infantry regiments between them, along with supporting elements. Even making up six full strength units in the two brigades involved pulling elements from three other armoured regiments and five other infantry battalions. In addition to forces from BAOR, some additional units were dispatched from the UK. The division had much stronger supporting elements than a division in Germany had. Following the success of Operation GRANBY (US DESERT SHIELD and DESERT STORM) in 1991, the British forces returned to their peacetime stations. BAOR at this time was still around 54,000 personnel.

◻ *BAOR 1983—1990*

> Note: organizationally the entire period 1983—1993 could be covered in one section. However, combining ten years of rotations along with details of BAOR support for the first Gulf War (Operation GRANBY) and then the dissolution of BAOR itself at the end of the period produced a very cluttered listing. Therefore, the period was divided in two.

HQ BAOR   *Rheindahlen*

HQ 4th Signal Group   *Rheindahlen*
    13th Signal Regt (Radio)   *Birgelen*
    14th Signal Regt (EW)   *Celle*
    16th Signal Regt   *Krefeld*
    21st Signal Regt (Air Support)   *Lemgo*
    28th Signal Regt   *St Tonis*

40 Army Engineer Sp Regt[133] {43 Sp Sqn RE}   *Willich*
10 Field Sqn RE   *Gütersloh*
14 Topographic Sqn RE   *Mönchen-Gladbach*

12th Flight AAC   *Wildenrath (Bruggen?)*

HQ 1 (British) Corps   *Bielefeld*
7th Signal Regt   *Herford*
22nd Signal Regt (Air Formation)   *Lippstadt*
664th Sqn AAC   *Detmold*

▣ **Artillery Division** [▣ **1ˢᵗ Artillery Brigade** Nov 1985][134]
    Dortmund
50th Missile Regt RA   *Menden*
    15, 19, 36, 51 Msl Btys RA[135] [Lance SSM]
5th Heavy Regt RA   *Hildesheim*; moved 1984 to *Dortmund*
    K, P, 18 Hy Btys RA[136] [M110], Q Loc Bty RA

---

[133] Later redesignated as 40 Army Sp Group RE.
[134] The Artillery Division was redesignated 1984 as Artillery, 1 (British) Corps. On 1 Nov 1985, a new 1ˢᵗ Artillery Brigade was formed in BAOR as a tactical headquarters for GHQ artillery.
[135] 51 Msl Bty RA disbanded Jan 1985 and the remaining batteries increased from 3 to 4 Lance SSM launchers each.
[136] 18 Hy Bty RA left Jan 1985.

[Artillery Division/1st Artillery Brigade]
32nd Heavy Regt RA   *Dortmund*
         12, 25, 27, 46 Hy Btys RA[137] [M107]
39th Heavy Regt RA   *Sennelager*
         34, 56, 76 Hy Btys RA[138] [M107; Feb 1990 MLRS]
16th Air Defence Regt RA   *Dortmund*
         14, 30, 32 AD Btys RA [Rapier]
         replaced Aug 1985 by 12th AD Regiment RA {T, 9, 58 AD Btys
             RA[139]}
22nd Air Defence Regt RA   *Dortmund*
         11, 42, 53 AD Btys RA[140] [Rapier]
94th Locating Regt RA   *Celle*; moved to UK [Larkhill] 1985
         57, 73, 156 Loc Btys RA[141]
8th Artillery Support Regt RCT {5, 12, 13, 27 Sqns RCT}   *Munster*

23 Engineer Regt   *Osnabrück*
         25, 39, 73 Field Sqns and 43 Field Sp Sqn RE
28th Amphibious Engineer Regt   *Osnabrück*
         23, 64 Amphib Engr Sqns and 71 HQ Sqn RE
32nd Armoured Engineer Regt   *Hameln*
         26, 31, 77 Armd Sqns RE
25 Engineer Regt [established Jan 1985]   *Osnabrück*
         12 and 16 Field Sqns RE
65 Corps Sp Sqn RE   *Osnabrück* (or *Hameln*)

7th Tank Transporter Regt RCT {3, 16, 617 Sqns RCT}   *Bielefeld*
10th Regt RCT {9, 17, 36 Sqns RCT}   *Bielefeld*
5th Ordnance Bn   *location unknown*
6th Ordnance Bn   *location unknown*
9th Ordnance Bn   *location unknown*
I (Corps) Field Workshop REME   *Bielefeld*
70th Aircraft Workshop REME   *location unknown*

---

[137] 12 Hy Bty RA left Dec 1984 and replaced Jan 1985 by 18 Hy Bty RA, along with 57 Loc Bty RA.
[138] 76 Bty replaced by 132 Bty in Jul 1985. Reorganized with 132 and 176 Hy Btys RA when it converted to MLRS in Feb 1990.
[139] 12 AD Bty RA added Oct 1985; note that 12 was previously a Hy Bty RA in 32nd Regt.
[140] Added 35 AD Bty RA in Mar 1985.
[141] 57 Loc Bty RA left Dec 1984; reorganized Jan 1985 with 5, 22, 73, 156 Loc Btys RA.

⧉ 1st Armoured Division

1st Armoured Division HQ & Signal Regt   *Verden*
1st The Queen's Dragoon Guards [recce]   *Hohne*
        replaced Nov 1984 by 9th/12th Royal Lancers at *Wolfenbüttel*
        replaced Mar 1987 by 1st The Queen's Dragoon Guards
1st Regt RHA[142]   *Hohne*
        A, B, E Btys RHA   [Abbot]
45th Field Regt RA   *Hohne*
        52, 94, 170 Field Btys RA [M109]
        replaced Apr 1985 by 40th Field Regt RA[143] {38, 129, 137 Fd Btys RA}
4th Field Regt RA[144] [assigned Apr 1983]   *Osnabrück*
        29, 88, 97 Field Btys RA [M109]
10th AD Bty RA [Blowpipe]   *Hohne*
D Battery RHA [FV438 Swingfire]   *Hohne* [left ca. 1983]
21 Engineer Regt   *Nienburg*
        1, 4. 7 Field Sqns and 45 Field Sp Sqn RE
1st Regt AAC   *Hildesheim*
        651, 652, 661 Sqns AAC
1st Armoured Division Transport Regt   *Bunde*
        2, 4, 33 Sqns RCT; from Apr 1986 also 74 HQ Sqn RCT
1st Ordnance Bn   *location unknown*
1st Armoured Division REME {7 and 12 Workshops REME}
        location unknown
1st Armoured Division RAMC   *location unknown*

7th ARMOURED BRIGADE
12th ARMOURED BRIGADE
22nd ARMOURED BRIGADE

---

[142] From 1988 allotted for CS of 22nd Armoured Brigade.
[143] From 1988 allotted for CS of 7th Armoured Brigade.
[144] From 1988 allotted for CS of 12th Armoured Brigade.

🖾 3ʳᵈ **Armoured Division**

3ʳᵈ Armoured Division HQ & Signal Regt   *Soest*
9ᵗʰ/12ᵗʰ Lancers [recce]   UK [Wimbish]
        replaced 1984 by 1ˢᵗ Queen's Dragoon Guards
        replaced 1987 by 9ᵗʰ/12ᵗʰ Lancers
2ⁿᵈ Field Regt RA[145]   *Munster*
        L, N, O Field Btys RA [M109]
19ᵗʰ Field Regt RA[146]   *Dortmund*
        5, 13, 25, 28 Field Btys RA [Abbot
        replaced Aug 1990 by 27ᵗʰ Field Regt RA {6, 23, 49 Field Btys RA}
            [M109]
40ᵗʰ Field Regt RA   UK [Colchester][147]
        38, 129, 137 Field Btys RA [FH70]
        replaced Apr 1985 by 45ᵗʰ Field Regt RA {52, 94, 170 Field Btys RA}
        replaced Mar 1990 by 3ʳᵈ Regt RHA {C, D, J Btys RHA}
111ᵗʰ AD Bty RA [Blowpipe]   *location unknown*
        replaced 1985 by 46ᵗʰ AD Bty RA at *Dortmund*
J Battery RHA [FV438 Swingfire]   *Paderborn* [left ca. 1983]
26 Engineer Regt   *Iserlohn*
        5, 25, 30 Field Sqns and 2 Field Sp Sqn RE
3ʳᵈ Regt AAC   *Soest*
        653, 662, 663 Sqns AAC
3ʳᵈ Armoured Division Transport Regt   *Duisberg*
        6, 21, 35 Sqns RCT, 75 HQ Sqn RCT
3ʳᵈ Ordnance Bn   *location unknown*
3ʳᵈ Armoured Division REME: 6 and 11 Workshops REME   *location unknown*
3ʳᵈ Armoured Division RAMC   *location unknown*

4ᵗʰ Aʀᴍᴏᴜʀᴇᴅ Bʀɪɢᴀᴅᴇ
6ᵗʰ Aʀᴍᴏᴜʀᴇᴅ/Aɪʀᴍᴏʙɪʟᴇ/Aʀᴍᴏᴜʀᴇᴅ Bʀɪɢᴀᴅᴇ
19ᵗʰ Iɴꜰᴀɴᴛʀʏ Bʀɪɢᴀᴅᴇ [Colchester, UK] to 31 Mar 1986
from 1 Apr 1986, 33ʳᵈ Aʀᴍᴏᴜʀᴇᴅ Bʀɪɢᴀᴅᴇ

---

[145] Allotted from 1988 for CS of 4ᵗʰ Armoured Brigade.
[146] Allotted 1988 for CS of 6ᵗʰ Armoured [Airmobile] Brigade.
[147] It appears that even after the UK-based 19ᵗʰ Infantry Brigade was transferred to 4ᵗʰ Armoured Division in 1986, 3ʳᵈ Armoured Division continued to have a field regiment RA stationed there. However, 3ʳᵈ Regt RHA in 4ᵗʰ Armoured Division has been shown as allotted for CS of 33ʳᵈ Armoured Brigade from 1988, even though that brigade was no longer assigned to the division.

▨ 4th Armoured Division

4th Armoured Division HQ & Signal Regt   *Herford*
15th/19th Hussars [recce]   *Paderborn* [left Nov 1984]
          replaced Jan 1985 by 13th/18th Kings Royal Hussars at *Herford*
          replaced Jan 1987 by 16th/5th Queens Royal Lancers
25th Field Regt RA   *Paderborn*
          35, 54, 93 Field Btys RA [Abbot]
          replaced Apr 1984 by 3rd Regt RHA[148] {C, D, J Btys RHA}
          replaced Feb 1990 by 45th Field Regt RA {52, 94, 170 Fd Btys RA}
               [M109]
27th Field Regt RA   *Lippstadt*
          6, 23, 49 Field Btys RA [M109]
          replaced Apr 1986 by 49th Field Regt RA[149] {55, 127, 143 Fd Btys RA}
47th Field Regt RA[150] *Gütersloh*
          3, 4, 31 Field Btys RA [Abbot]
          replaced Apr 1989 by 26th Field Regt RA {16, 17, 159 Field Btys RA}
               [M109]
43rd AD Bty RA [Blowpipe]   *Gütersloh*
C Battery RHA [FV438 Swingfire]   *Gütersloh* [left ca.1983]
35 Engineer Regt   *Hameln*
          27, 29, 42 Field Sqns and 44 Field Sp Sqn RE
4th Regt AAC   *Detmold*
          654, 659, 669 Sqns AAC
4th Armoured Division Transport Regt   *Minden*
          11, 19 Sqns RCT, 76 HQ Sqn RCT [plus one Sqn in Colchester]
4th Ordnance Battalion   *location unknown*
4th Armoured Division REME: 4 and 5 Workshops REME   *location unknown*
4th Armoured Division RAMC   *location unknown*

11th ARMOURED BRIGADE
20th ARMOURED BRIGADE
33rd ARMOURED BRIGADE until 31 Mar 1986[151]
19th INFANTRY BRIGADE [Colchester, UK] from 1 Apr 1986

---

[148] Formed Apr 1984 from personnel and equipment of 25th Field Regiment RA.
[149] Allotted 1988 for CS of 20th Armoured Brigade.
[150] Allotted 1988 for CS of 11th Armoured Brigade.
[151] On 1 Apr 1986 this brigade went to 3rd Armoured Division, and 4th Armoured Division took over 19th Infantry Brigade in Colchester.

BRIGADES

4ᵗʰ Armoured Brigade
HQ & 204ᵗʰ Signal Sqn   *Munster*
Queen's Royal Irish Hussars   *Munster*
          replaced Mar 1988 by 14ᵗʰ/20ᵗʰ King's Royal Hussars
17ᵗʰ/21ˢᵗ Lancers   *Munster*
          replaced Dec 1990 by Royal Hussars
1ˢᵗ Bn Irish Guards   *Munster*
          replaced Jan 1986 by 1ˢᵗ Bn Grenadier Guards[152]

6ᵗʰ Armoured Brigade [Nov 1983 to Jan 1988, **6ᵗʰ Airmobile Brigade**]
HQ & 206ᵗʰ Signal Sqn   *Soest*
3ʳᵈ Royal Tank Regt [arrived Feb 1988]   *Hemer*
1ˢᵗ Bn Worcestershire & Sherwood Foresters Regt   *Hemer*
          replaced Oct 1984 by 1ˢᵗ Bn Gordon Highlanders
          replaced Mar 1988 by 1ˢᵗ Bn QO Highlanders
          replaced Dec 1988 by 1ˢᵗ Bn Royal Scots at *Werl*
1ˢᵗ Bn Light Infantry   *Hemer*
          replaced Dec 1984 by 2ⁿᵈ Bn Light Infantry
          replaced Mar 1988 by 3ʳᵈ Bn Royal Regt of Fusiliers

7ᵗʰ Armoured Brigade
HQ & 207ᵗʰ Signal Sqn   *Soltau*
Royal Hussars[153]   *Soltau*
          replaced Nov 1988 by Royal Scots Dragoon Guards
14ᵗʰ/20ᵗʰ King's Hussars   *Hohne*
          replaced May 1985 by 2ⁿᵈ Royal Tank Regt
          replaced Mar 1990 by Queen's Royal Irish Hussars
3ʳᵈ Bn Queen's Regt   *Fallingbostel*
          replaced Jan 1986 by 1ˢᵗ Bn Staffordshire Regt

---

[152] The first battalion mounted in the Warrior Infantry Fighting Vehicle.
[153] First regiment to convert to Challenger tanks, 1983. They lingered at Soltau until around Jan 1989.

▣ **11th Armoured Brigade**

211 HQ & Signal Sqn   *Minden*

3rd Royal Tank Regt   *Munster* [left Jan 1986]

5th R Inniskilling Dragoon Guards [arrived Nov 1986]   *Paderborn*

1st Bn Royal Regt of Fusiliers   *Minden*
        replaced Feb 1986 3rd Bn Royal Anglian Regt
        replaced Jan 1989 by 1st Bn Argyll & Sutherland Highlanders

2nd Bn Royal Green Jackets   *Minden*
        replaced Mar 1986 by 2nd Bn Queen's Regt

▣ **12th Armoured Brigade**

212 HQ & Signal Sqn   *Osnabrück*

5th Royal Inniskilling Dragoon Guards   *Osnabrück*
        replaced Nov 1984 by 4th Royal Tank Regt

1st Bn King's Regt   *Osnabrück*
        replaced 1985 by 1st Bn Royal Irish Rangers
        replaced Jul 1990 by 1st Bn POWO Regt of Yorkshire

1st Bn KO Scottish Borderers   *Osnabrück* [left Feb 1984]

1st Bn Green Howards [assigned Jan 1983]   *Osnabrück*
        replaced Apr 1987 by 1st Bn Royal Green Jackets

▣ **20th Armoured Brigade**

HQ & 200th Signal Sqn   *Detmold*

Life Guards   *Detmold*
        replaced Jan 1984 by Blues and Royals
        replaced Jan 1990 by 15th/19th Hussars

4th/7th Royal Dragoon Guards [arrived Apr 1983]*Detmold*

1st Bn Royal Regt of Wales   *Lemgo*
        replaced Aug 1988 by 2nd Bn Royal Irish Rangers

▣ **22nd Armoured Brigade**

HQ & 201st Signal Sqn   *Hohne*

2nd Royal Tank Regt   *Hohne* [left May 1985]
        replaced Oct 1984 by 1st Royal Tank Regt at *Hildesheim*

14th/20th Hussars   *Hohne*
        replaced May 1985 by Queen's Own Hussars[154]

1st Bn Welsh Guards [arrived Feb 1984]   *Fallingbostel*
        replaced Feb 1988 by 1st Bn Scots Guards

---

[154] The last regiment to convert to Challenger tanks, in 1989.

[22nd Armoured Brigade]
        3rd Bn Royal Green Jackets   *Celle*
            replaced Mar 1987 by 2nd Bn Royal Anglian Regt

▭* **33rd Armoured Brigade**
        HQ & 202nd Signal Sqn   *Paderborn*
        Royal Scots Dragoon Guards   *Sennelager*
            replaced Nov 1986 by 15th/19th Hussars
            replaced Jan 1990 by Life Guards
        1st Bn Royal Highland Fusiliers   *Hemer*
            replaced Nov 1984 by 1st Bn Queen's Lancashire Regt at
                Paderborn
            replaced Feb 1990 by 3rd Bn Light Infantry
        1st Bn Black Watch   *Werl*
            replaced Mar 1985 1st Bn Royal Scots
            replaced Dec 1988 by 1st Bn QO Highlanders at *Munster*

⊠* **19th Infantry Brigade**[155]
HQ & 209th Signal Sqn   Colchester
3rd Bn Royal Anglian Regt   Colchester
        replaced Feb 1984 by 1st Bn King's Own Scottish Borderers
        replaced Mar 1987 by 3rd Bn Royal Green Jackets
        replaced Feb 1989 by 3rd Bn Royal Anglian Regt
1st Bn Devonshire and Dorset Regt   Colchester
        replaced Apr 1983 by 2nd Bn Royal Anglian Regt
        replaced Feb 1987 by 1st Bn King's Own Royal Border Regt
2nd Bn Queen's Regt   Colchester
        replaced Jan 1983 by 1st Bn Staffordshire Regt
        replaced Jan 1986 by 1st Bn Argyll and Sutherland Highlanders
        replaced Jan 1989 by 2nd Bn Royal Anglian Regt

---

[155] Although based in the UK, assigned 1982 to 3rd Armoured Division and switched 1986 to 4th Armoured Division.

⊠ **2ⁿᵈ Infantry Division**[156]

2ⁿᵈ Infantry Division HQ & Signal Regiment   York
1ˢᵗ Field Regt RHA   Topcliffe[157]
       A, B, E Btys RHA [FH70]
       replaced Apr 1982 by 49ᵗʰ Field Regt RA {53, 127, 143 Fd Btys RA}
       replaced Apr 1986 by 27ᵗʰ Field Regt RA {6, 23, 49 Fd Btys RA}
       replaced Aug 1990 by 3ʳᵈ Field Regt RHA {C, D, J Btys RHA}
9ᵗʰ Regt AAC [reformed Jun 1989]   Dishforth

⊠ **24ᵗʰ Infantry/Airmobile Brigade**[158]
HQ & 210ᵗʰ Signal Sqn   Catterick
1ˢᵗ Bn Duke of Wellington's Regt   Catterick
       replaced Dec 1983 by 2ⁿᵈ Bn Royal Regt of Fusiliers
       replaced Dec 1987 by 1ˢᵗ Bn Prince of Wales's Own Regt of Yorkshire
       replaced Jul 1990 by 1ˢᵗ Bn Duke of Edinburgh's Royal Regt
1ˢᵗ Bn Green Howards   Catterick
       replaced Mar 1983 by 1ˢᵗ Bn KOR Border Regt
       replaced May 1985 by 3ʳᵈ Bn Royal Regt of Fusiliers
       replaced Nov 1988 by 1ˢᵗ Bn Green Howards
1ˢᵗ Bn Gloucestershire Regt [assigned Feb 1990]   Catterick
51 Field Sqn RE   Catterick

⊠ **15ᵗʰ (North East) Infantry Brigade**[159]
       Queen's Own Yeomanry
       6ᵗʰ (V) Bn Royal Regiment of Fusiliers
       1ˢᵗ Bn Yorkshire Volunteers
       2ⁿᵈ Bn Yorkshire Volunteers
       7ᵗʰ (V) Bn Light Infantry
       4ᵗʰ (V) Bn Parachute Regt
       101ˢᵗ (Northumbrian) Field Regt RA (V)
          203, 204, 205 Fd Btys RA (V)

---

[156] Division headquarters relocated to the UK Jan 1983 and was redesignated from armoured division to infantry division.
[157] The artillery regiment at Topcliffe is also sometimes shown as part of 24ᵗʰ Brigade.
[158] The brigade was redesignated Apr 1988 as 24ᵗʰ Airmobile Brigade.
[159] Territorial Army brigade established Jan 1982 with headquarters at Topcliffe.

⊠ **49th (East) Infantry Brigade**[160]
       The Royal Yeomanry
       5th (V) Bn Royal Regiment of Fusiliers
       5th (V) Bn Royal Anglian Regt
       7th (V) Bn Royal Anglian Regt
       1st Bn Mercian Volunteers
       5th (V) Bn Light Infantry
       100th (Yeomanry) Field Regt RA (V)
              200, 201, 202 Field Btys RA (V)

---

[160] Territorial Army brigade established 1982 with headquarters at Nottingham.

▱ *BAOR 1990—1994*

> Note: This section begins approximately late spring 1990.

HQ BAOR   *Rheindahlen* [closed Mar 1994]

HQ 4th Signal Group   *Rheindahlen* [disbanded Jul 1992]
     13th Signal Regt (Radio)   *Birgelen*
     14th Signal Regt (EW)   *Celle*
     16th Signal Regt   *Krefeld*
     21st Signal Regt (Air Support)   *Lemgo* [moved to UK May 1992]
     28th Signal Regt   *St Tonis* [reduced to 280th Signal Sqn 1994]

40 Army Sp Group {43 Sp Sqn RE}   *Willich* [disbanded 1992]
10 Field Sqn RE   *Gütersloh* [disbanded 1992]
14 Topographic Sqn RE   *Mönchen-Gladbach*

12th Flight AAC   *Wildenrath (Bruggen?)*

24th Transport & Movements Regt RCT   *Hanover* [Merged into 24th Sp
     Regt RLC]
25th Transport & Movements Regt RCT   *Bielefeld* [Merged into 24th Sp
     Regt RLC]
26th Transport & Movements Regt RCT   *location unknown* [disbanded]
14th Sqn RCT   *Bielefeld*
54th Engineer & Ambulance Sqn RCT   *Lubbecke* [disbanded]
68th Sqn RCT   *Rheindahlen*
79th Railway Sqn RCT   *location unknown* [moved to UK ca. 1993]

Wahrendorf Petrol Depot RAOC   *Wahrendorf* [merged into 14th
     Regiment RLC]
15th Ordnance Group   *Wulfen* [merged into 15th Regiment RLC]
16th Ordnance Bn RAOC   *location unknown* [moved to UK and
     became16th Regiment RLC]
154th Forward Ammunition Depot RAOC   *location unknown* [merged
     into 12th Regiment RLC]

71st Aircraft Workshop REME   Minden [disbanded 1994]
20th Corps Electrical Workshop REME   *Minden* [disbanded]
23rd Base Workshop REME   *Wetter* [disbanded]
37th (Rhine) Workshop REME   *location unknown* [disbanded 1991-2]

HQ 1 (British) Corps   *Bielefeld* [closed Oct 1992; basis for HQ ARRC]
7th Signal Regt   *Herford*
22nd Signal Regt (Air Formation)   *Lippstadt* [disbanded Sep 1992]
664th Sqn AAC   *Detmold*

1st Artillery Brigade[161]   *Dortmund* [disbanded ca. 1993]
50th Missile Regt RA   *Menden* [disbanded Mar 1993]
     15, 19, 36 Msl Btys RA [Lance SSM]
5th Heavy Regt RA   *Dortmund*
     K, P Hy Btys RA [M110; MLRS Jan 1992], Q Loc Bty RA
32nd Heavy Regt RA   *Dortmund* [moved to UK Nov 1993]
     18, 25, 27, 46 Hy Btys RA[162] [M107; MLRS 1992]; 57 Loc Bty RA
39th Heavy Regt RA[163]   *Sennelager*
     132, 176 Hy Btys RA [MLRS]
12th Air Defence Regt RA   *Dortmund*
     T, 9, 12, 58 AD Btys RA [Rapier]
22nd Air Defence Regt RA   *Dortmund* [left Aug 1992]
     11, 42, 35, 53 AD Btys RA [Rapier]
16th Air Defence Regt RA [arrived Jun 1992]   *Dortmund*
     14, 30, 32 AD Btys RA [Rapier; Javelin in 14 Bty]
8th Artillery Support Regt RCT   *Munster* [moved to UK 1993]
     5, 12, 13, 27 Sqns RCT

23 Engineer Regt   *Munster* [disbanded 1993]
     25, 39, 73 Field Sqns and 43 Field Sp Sqn RE
28th Amphibious Engineer Regt   *Osnabrück*[164]
     23, 64 Amphib Engr Sqns and 71 HQ Sqn RE
32nd Armoured Engineer Regt   *Hameln*; Sep 1993 to *Hohne*
     26, 31, 77 Armd Sqns RE
25 Engineer Regt   *Osnabrück* [disbanded 1992]
     12 and 16 Field Sqns RE
65 Corps Sp Sqn RE   *Osnabrück*

---

[161] 94th Locating Regt RA, in the UK (Larkhill) was still earmarked for BAOR.
[162] The regiment was reorganized with 18 and 74 Hy Btys RA when it converted to MLRS in 1991, along with 57 Loc Bty RA.
[163] Served in Desert Storm 1990-91 under 1st Armoured Division.
[164] Reorganized during 1993, which included taking over 65 Corps Sp Sqn RE.

7th Tank Transporter Regt RCT {3, 16, 617 Sqns RCT}   *Bielefeld*
10th Regt RCT {9, 17, 36 Sqns RCT}   *Bielefeld*

5th Ordnance Bn   *location unknown* [disbanded 1993]
6th Ordnance Bn   *location unknown* [merged into 6th Supply Regt RLC]
9th Ordnance Bn   *location unknown* [moved to UK and merged into 9th
      Supply Regt RLC]

1 Corps Field Workshop REME   *Bielefeld* [merged into 2nd Bn REME]
70th Aircraft Workshop REME   *location unknown* [moved to UK (Wattisham)
      1994]

▱▱ 1st Armoured Division

1st Armoured Division HQ & Signal Regt[165]   *Verden*
1st The Queen's Dragoon Guards [recce]   *Wolfenbüttel*
      replaced Jul 1991 by 13th/18th Hussars
      replaced Oct 1992 by Light Dragoons[166]
45th Field Regt RA   *Hohne*
      34, 52, 170 Field Btys RA [M109]
      replaced Apr 1985 by 40th Field Regt RA[167] {38, 129, 137 Field Btys
          RA}
1st Regt RHA   *Hohne* [moved to the UK Jun 1993]
      A, B, E Btys RHA   [Abbot]
4th Field Regt RA   *Osnabrück* [left Sep 1994]
      29, 88, 97 Field Btys RA [M109]
40th Field Regt RA   *Hohne* [left Oct 1994]
      38, 129, 173 Field Btys RA [M109]
21 Engineer Regt   *Nienburg*
      1, 4. 7 Field Sqns and 45 Field Sp Sqn RE
1st Regt AAC   *Hildesheim*
      651, 652, 661 Sqns AAC
1st Armoured Division Transport Regt   *Bunde* [merged into 1st Regt RLC]
      2, 4, 33 Sqns RCT; from Apr 1986 also 74 HQ Sqn RCT

---

[165] This formed the command element for British Army forces in Operation GRANBY
(US DESERT SHIELD/DESERT STORM) 1990-91. The division was disbanded Dec 1992
and its HQ redesignated HQ Lower Saxony District; that headquarters was itself
disbanded Nov 1993.
[166] 13th/18th Hussars and 15th/19th Hussars amalgamated 1 Dec 1992 at this station as
The Light Dragoons.
[167] Served in Desert Storm 1990-91 under 1st Armoured Division.

[1st Armoured Division]
1st Ordnance Bn   *location unknown* [merged into 1st Regt RLC]
1st Armoured Division REME {7 and 12 Workshops REME}
          location unknown [merged into 1st Bn REME]
1st Armoured Division RAMC   *location(s) unknown*

7th ARMOURED BRIGADE
12th ARMOURED BRIGADE
22nd ARMOURED BRIGADE

3rd Armoured Division

3rd Armoured Division HQ & Signal Regt   *Soest*[168]
9th/12th Lancers [recce]   UK [Wimbish]
          replaced Jul 1991 by 16th/5th Lancers [relieved Jun 1993]
2nd Field Regt RA[169]   *Dortmund* [disbanded Dec 1993]
          L, N, O Field Btys RA [M109]
19th Field Regt RA   *Dortmund*
          13, 25, 28 Field Btys RA [Abbot]
          replaced Aug 1990 by 27th Field Regt RA: 6, 23, 49 Field Btys RA
                    [M109] which left Mar 1993
40th Field Regt RA   UK [Colchester]
          38, 129, 137 Field Btys RA [FH70]
26 Engineer Regt   *Iserlohn* [disbanded Jul 1994]
          5, 25, 30 Field Sqns and 2 Field Sp Sqn RE
3rd Regt AAC   *Soest* [moved to the UK 1993]
          653, 662, 663 Sqns AAC
3rd Armoured Division Transport Regt   *Duisberg* [moved to the UK
                    and merge into 3rd Regt RLC]
          6, 21, 35 Sqns RCT, 75 HQ Sqn RCT
3rd Ordnance Bn   *location unknown* [moved to the UK and merge into 3rd
          Regt RLC]
3rd Armoured Division REME: 6 and 11 Workshops REME   *location
          unknown* [merged into 3rd Bn REME]
3rd Armoured Division RAMC   *location unknown* [moved to the UK?]

4th ARMOURED BRIGADE
6th ARMOURED BRIGADE
33rd ARMOURED BRIGADE

---

[168] The division was dissolved in Germany and HQ reestablished in the UK (Bulford)
Oct 1993 as 3rd (UK) Division.
[169] Served in Desert Storm 1990-91 under 1st Armoured Division.

⊡ 4th Armoured Division

4th Armoured Division HQ & Signal Regt   *Herford*[170]

16th/5th Queens Royal Lancers [recce]   *Herford*
     replaced Jul 1991 by 9th/12th Royal Lancers [left Jul 1994]

45th Field Regt RA   *Paderborn* [disbanded Jun 1993]
     52, 94, 170 Field Btys RA [M109]

27th Field Regt RA   *Lippstadt*
     6, 23, 49 Field Btys RA [M109]
     replaced Apr 1986 by 49th Field Regt RA {55, 127, 143 Fd Btys RA}
       [disbanded Aug 1992]

26th Field Regt RA   *Gütersloh* [left Jul 1994]
     16, 17, 159 Field Btys RA [M109]

35 Engineer Regt   *Hameln*
     29, 27, 42 Field Sqns and 44 Field Sp Sqn RE

4th Regt AAC: 654, 659, 669 Sqns AAC   *Detmold*

4th Armoured Division Transport Regt   *Minden* [moved to UK and
     merged into 4th Regt RLC]
     11, 19 Sqns RCT, 76 HQ Sqn RCT [plus one Sqn in Colchester]

4th Ordnance Battalion   *location unknown* [moved to UK and merged
     into 4th Regt RLC]

4th Armoured Division REME: 4 and 5 Workshops REME   *location
     unknown* [merged into 2nd Bn REME]

4th Armoured Division RAMC   *location unknown*

11th ARMOURED BRIGADE

20th ARMOURED BRIGADE

19th INFANTRY BRIGADE [Colchester, UK]

---

[170] In Jul 1993 this became the new 1st Armoured Division HQ and Signal Regt.

BRIGADES

◻ **4th Armoured Brigade**
        HQ & 204th Signal Sqn[171]   *Munster*
        14th/20th King's Royal Hussars[172]   *Munster*
            replaced Dec 1992 by The King's Royal Hussars[173]
        17th/21st Lancers   *Munster*
            replaced Dec 1990 by The Royal Hussars [left Dec 1992]
        1st Bn Grenadier Guards[174]   *Munster*
            replaced Nov 1991 by 1st Bn Coldstream Guards

◻ **6th Armoured Brigade**
        HQ & 206th Signal Sqn   *Soest* [disbanded Sep 1992]
        3rd Royal Tank Regt   *Hemer* [left Jun 1992]
        1st Bn Royal Scots[175]   *Werl*
            replaced Aug 1991 by 1st Bn Devonshire & Dorset Regt
        3rd Bn Royal Regt of Fusiliers[176]   *Hemer* [disbanded Jul 1992]

◻ **7th Armoured Brigade**
        HQ & 207th Signal Sqn[177]   *Soltau*
        Royal Scots Dragoon Guards[178]   *Soltau*
            replaced Jul 1992 by 2nd Royal Tank Regt

---

[171] Served in the Gulf 1990-91, under 1st Armoured Division. 4th Armoured Brigade disbanded at Munster Jan 1993 and reformed at Osnabrück from 12th Armoured Brigade.

[172] Served in the Gulf 1990-91, under 4th Armoured Brigade; reinforced by 'A' Sqn The Life Guards and elements 4th RTR.

[173] The Royal Hussars and 14th/20th King's Hussars amalgamated 4 Dec 1992 at this station to form The King's Royal Hussars.

[174] The first battalion mounted in the Warrior Infantry Fighting Vehicle.

[175] Served in the Gulf 1990-91 under 4th Armoured Brigade; reinforced with Queen's Coy 1st Bn Grenadier Guards and elements 1st Bn Queen's Own Highlanders.

[176] Served in the Gulf 1990-91 under 4th Armoured Brigade; reinforced with No 2 Coy 1st Bn Grenadier Guards and elements 1st Bn Queen's Own Highlanders.

[177] Served in the Gulf 1990-91. 7th Armoured Brigade disbanded at Soltau Feb 1993 and reformed Apr 1993 at Hohne from 22nd Armoured Brigade.

[178] Served in the Gulf 1990-91 under 7th Armoured Brigade; reinforced by elements of 14th/20th King's Hussars, 17th/21st Lancers, and 4th RTR.

[7th Armoured Brigade]
      Queen's Royal Irish Hussars[179]   *Hohne*
          replaced Sep 1993 by Queen's Royal Hussars
      1st Bn Staffordshire Regt[180]   *Fallingbostel*
          replaced Nov 1991 by 1st Bn Cheshire Regt [left Jun 1993]

11th Armoured Brigade
      211 HQ & Signal Sqn   *Minden* [disbanded Jan 1993]
      5th R Inniskilling Dragoon Gds[181]   *Paderborn* [left Jul 1992]
      1st Bn Argyll & Sutherland Highlanders   *Minden* [left Jun
          1993]
      2nd Bn Queen's Regt   *Minden*
          replaced Jan 1991 by 1st Bn Queen's Regt [left Jun 1992]

12th Armoured Brigade
      212 HQ & Signal Sqn   *Osnabrück*[182]
      4th Royal Tank Regt   *Osnabrück* [left Jul 1993]
      1st Bn Royal Irish Rangers   *Osnabrück*
          replaced Jul 1990 by 1st Bn POWO Regt of Yorkshire
      1st Bn Royal Green Jackets   *Osnabrück*
          replaced Jul 1991 by 1st Bn Duke of Wellington's Regt [left
          Jun 1993]

20th Armoured Brigade
      HQ & 200th Signal Sqn[183]   *Detmold*
      15th/19th Hussars   *Detmold* [left Dec 1992]

---

[179] Served in the Gulf 1990-91 under 7th Armoured Brigade; reinforced by elements 17th/21st Lancers. On 1 Sep 1993 The Queen's Royal Irish Hussars amalgamated with The Queen's Own Hussars at this station to form The Queen's Royal Hussars (The Queen's Own and Royal Irish).
[180] Served in the Gulf 1990-91 under 7th Armoured Brigade; reinforced by elements of 1st Bn Grenadier Guards, 2nd Bn Royal Anglian Regiment, 1st Bn Prince of Wales's Own Regiment of Yorkshire, and 1st Bn Royal Green Jackets.
[181] Moved 1 Aug 1992 to Detmold and amalgamated with 4th/7th Royal Dragoon Guards as The Royal Dragoon Guards.
[182] Redesignated Jan 1993 as HQ & 204th Signal Sqn to reform 4th Armoured Brigade.
[183] Disbanded Dec 1992 and 20th Armoured Brigade dissolved at Detmold. Reformed at Paderborn from 33rd Armoured Brigade.

[20th Armoured Brigade]
>>>>> 4th/7th Royal Dragoon Gds[184]   *Detmold*
>>>>>   replaced Jul 1992 by Royal Dragoon Gds
>>>>> 2nd Bn Royal Irish Rangers[185]   *Lemgo* [left Jul 1993]

22nd Armoured Brigade
>>>>> HQ & 201st Signal Sqn[186]   *Hohne*
>>>>> Queen's Own Hussars[187]   *Hohne* [left Aug 1993]
>>>>> 1st Royal Tank Regt   *Hildesheim*
>>>>> 1st Bn Scots Guards[188]   *Fallingbostel*
>>>>>   replaced Jun 1993 by 1st Bn Royal Highland Fusiliers
>>>>> 2nd Bn Royal Anglian Regt   *Celle*

33rd Armoured Brigade
>>>>> HQ & 202nd Signal Sqn[189]   *Paderborn*
>>>>> Life Guards[190]   *Sennelager*
>>>>>   replaced Sep 1992 by 1st Queen's Dragoon Guards
>>>>> 1st Bn Queen's Own Highlanders[191]   *Munster* [left Oct 1993]
>>>>> 3rd Bn Light Infantry   *Paderborn* [left Dec 1992]

19th Infantry Brigade[192]
>>>>> HQ & 209th Signal Sqn   Colchester
>>>>> 9th/12th Royal Lancers [recce]
>>>>>   replaced Jul 1991 by 16th/5th Queen's Royal Lancers
>>>>> 1st Bn Royal Anglian Regt   Colchester

---

[184] On 1 Aug 1992 the 4th/7th Royal Dragoon Guards and 5th Royal Inniskilling Dragoon Guards were amalgamated at this station as The Royal Dragoon Guards.

[185] Redesignated Jun 1992 as 2nd Bn Royal Irish Regt.

[186] Redesignated Apr 1993 as HQ & 207th Signal Sqn to reform 7th Armoured Brigade.

[187] The last regiment to convert to Challenger tanks, in 1989.

[188] Served in the Gulf 1990-91 as a Warrior delivery/reinforcement unit.

[189] Redesignated Dec 1992 as HQ and 200th Signal Sqn to reform 20th Armoured Brigade.

[190] Served in the Gulf 1990-91 as a tank delivery/reinforcement unit, less 'A' Sqn which served with 14th/20th King's Hussars. In Oct 1992 the Life Guards and Blues and Royals were effectively merged as The Household Cavalry Regiment.

[191] Served in the Gulf 1990-91 on lines of communications security duties.

[192] Although based in the UK, assigned 1982 to 3rd Armoured Division and switched 1986 to 4th Armoured Division. Relocated 1 Apr 1993 to Catterick, redesignated 19th Mechanised Brigade, and severed the connection with BAOR..

[19th Infantry Brigade]
        3rd Bn Royal Anglian Regt   Colchester
               replaced Apr 1991 by 1st Bn Royal Hampshire Regt[193]
        1st Bn King's Own Royal Border Regt   Colchester [left Jun 1992 w/o
               replacement]
        2nd Bn Royal Anglian Regt   Colchester

⊠ 2nd Infantry Division

2nd Infantry Division HQ & Signal Regiment   York
1st Field Regt RHA   Topcliffe[194]
        A, B, E Btys RHA [FH70]
        replaced Apr 1982 by 49th Field Regt RA {53, 127, 143 Fd Btys RA}
        replaced Apr 1986 by 27th Field Regt RA {6, 23, 49 Fd Btys RA}
        replaced Aug 1990 by 3rd Regt RHA {C, D, J Btys RHA}
9th Regt AAC   Dishforth

⊠ 24th Airmobile Brigade

HQ & 210th Signal Sqn   Catterick
1st Bn POWO Regt of Yorkshire   Catterick
        replaced Jul 1990 by 1st Bn Duke of Edinburgh's Royal Regt
1st Bn Green Howards   Catterick
1st Bn Gloucestershire Regt   Catterick
3rd Regt RHA [FH70   Topcliffe
51 Field Sqn RE   Catterick
9th Regt AAC   Dishforth

⊠ 15th (North East) Infantry Brigade[195]

        Queen's Own Yeomanry
        6th (V) Bn Royal Regiment of Fusiliers
        1st Bn Yorkshire Volunteers
        2nd Bn Yorkshire Volunteers
        7th (V) Bn Light Infantry
        4th (V) Bn Parachute Regt
        101st (Northumbrian) Field Regt RA (V)
             203, 204, 205 Fd Btys RA (V)

---

[193] Battalion redesignated Aug 1992 as 1st Bn Princess of Wales's Royal Regiment.
[194] The artillery regiment at Topcliffe is also sometimes shown as part of 24th Brigade.
[195] Territorial Army brigade with headquarters at Topcliffe.

⊠ **49th (East) Infantry Brigade**[196]
    The Royal Yeomanry
    5th (V) Bn Royal Regiment of Fusiliers
    5th (V) Bn Royal Anglian Regt
    7th (V) Bn Royal Anglian Regt
    1st Bn Mercian Volunteers
    5th (V) Bn Light Infantry
    100th (Yeomanry) Field Regt RA (V)
        200, 201, 202 Field Btys RA (V)

---

[196] Territorial Army brigade with headquarters at Chilwell.

Reinforcements

▲▲▲ BAOR generally held the major portion of the Royal Armoured Corps—especially of the tank regiments—and most (until fairly recent times, all) of the infantry battalions mounted in APCs. While always slated to receive individual reinforcements and support units, there was often little in the way of formed units in the UK suitable for mechanised war on the continent. 16th Parachute Brigade, in Germany in 1948 and then nominally based in the UK from 1949, constituted a potential reserve. However, it was often deployed elsewhere; even while in the UK it is not clear if it was ever tasked for Germany, and its parachute battalions would be a questionable choice for mobile warfare in the north German plain in any case. Generally, there were few regular brigades of any sort in the UK from the end of World War II into the 1960s. 3rd Infantry Division had been reformed in 1951 as a strategic reserve, but it was more often than not found in the Middle East. 6th Armoured Division was formed the same year, also for a strategic reserve role, but was then sent to Germany in 1952.

3rd Infantry Division was reformed 1959 in the UK to control units there (other than 16th Parachute Brigade Group) which were available for meeting overseas emergencies. It initially had 1st Guards and 19th Infantry Brigade Groups and 2nd Infantry Brigade. There were various changes in the assigned brigades in the following years; 1st Guards became 51st Infantry Brigade and later 51st Gurkha Brigade. When 51st Gurkha Brigade went to the Far East in 1964, 5th Infantry Brigade (as discussed earlier) moved from Germany to the UK in 1964 to help reform the strategic reserve. Barely 18 months later, that brigade headquarters was sent to Borneo (Sarawak) in Oct 1965 during the confrontation with Indonesia, remaining there for a year. 2nd Infantry Brigade left the division in 1966, but 24th Infantry Brigade joined it in 1967 after leaving Aden. The division also had recce and armoured regiments, a medium regiment RA, a light air defence regiment RA, and normal divisional troops.

6th Infantry Brigade went from Germany to the UK in Jan 1968, more as an economy measure than as a reserve, lingering through 1970 and then returning to BAOR as an armoured brigade.

On 1 Apr 1968 the Army Strategic Command was formed. It had the 3rd Infantry Division (5th, 19th and 24th Infantry Brigades). The brigades were later redesignated as airportable instead of infantry, and that designation suggested their nature: these were not mechanised formations. 5th Infantry Division was reborn Apr 1968 as well (2nd, 8th and 39th Infantry Brigades), but these were little more than holding units for battalions resting in the UK between operational commitments. 16th Parachute Brigade was also part of the new Command. Some other brigades could be found in the UK from time to time, but their intended wartime assignments (if any) are unknown. 5th Infantry Division was disbanded in 1970. The 8th Infantry Brigade would join the 39th Infantry Brigade in Ulster in 1971 as the troubles there pulled in larger numbers of British Army units, and 2nd Infantry Brigade was disbanded the same year.

The Territorial Army was, at least originally, a source of new units for BAOR should a war last long enough for them to be mobilized, properly trained and equipped, and then sent to Germany. The TA was set up in 1947 with two armoured divisions (49th and 56th), an airborne division (16th) and six infantry divisions (42nd, 43rd, 44th, 50th, 51st/52nd and 53rd) along with a few independent brigades.[197] In theory, these could be mobilized as in the two world wars and sent to Europe. By the end of 1955 only two divisions were still tasked as NATO reinforcements and the others remaining were organized for home defence. In 1956 the airborne division was eliminated (leaving behind a brigade group) and the two armoured divisions became infantry, while one more infantry division (54th) was created from two of the independent brigades. Further reductions in 1961 saw the elimination of the remaining (independent) armoured brigades. By the 1960s the staffing, training and equipment of the TA led at least some Regulars to question whether any part of it would be useful in the case of war. To them, the individuals and support units of the Army Emergency Reserve (AER) seemed of better use.

In Apr 1967 the whole TA was swept away, and only a few Volunteer units (part of a new Territorial Army and Volunteer Reserve, which incorporated the old AER) survived. These amounted to one armoured car regiment, the parachute brigade (three battalions), two SAS regiments, 13 infantry battalions, and five artillery regiments (two field and three air defence). There were also engineers, signals, and other supporting units. Other than the parachute brigade (44th) there were no tactical units above battalion in the new force. Presumably these units would be added into existing brigades on mobilization. (The only tactical headquarters, 44th Parachute Brigade, was disbanded in 1977.) The armoured car regiment was joined by a second in 1971. By the 1980s at least, perhaps eight TAVR battalions had a BAOR reinforcement role. There were increases in the number of infantry battalions in 1971 and 1975, and some more Yeomanry units were formed as well, albeit all with home defence roles. In Jan 1982 the 15th (North East) Brigade was formed at Topcliffe and the 49th (East) Brigade at Chilwell. These were operational rather than administrative brigades, coming under 2nd Infantry Division. Their mobilization role was to

---

[197] In 1950 the 51st/52nd (Scottish) Division was split into the 51st (Highland) and 52nd (Lowland) Divisions. All TA divisions (except for the 16th Airborne) also served as district headquarters.

move to Germany with 2nd Infantry Division for rear area security. In 1992 they lost their operational mission as part of the reductions under Options for Change.[198]

The regular divisions and brigades in the UK disappeared 1977, to be replaced by 6th Field Force (formed from HQ 16th Parachute Brigade), 7th Field Force (formed from HQ 19th Infantry Brigade) and 8th Field Force (formed from HQ 5th Infantry Brigade). These could contain both regular and volunteer battalions. 6th Field Force remained a sort of strategic reserve and intervention force (including a parachute element); 7th Field Force was tasked to reinforce BAOR; and 8th Field Force was for home defence. These reformed as brigades in 1982: 1st Infantry Brigade at Tidworth, 5th Infantry Brigade at Aldershot (with an airborne component), and 19th Infantry Brigade at Colchester. 24th Infantry Brigade disappeared in 1977, providing the headquarters for 5th Field Force in Germany. It reappeared Jan 1983 in the UK, coming under the new 2nd Infantry Division and given a BAOR reinforcement role[199]. By 1988 it was redesignated 24th Airmobile Brigade, taking over the role tested in Germany by 6th Armoured Brigade.[200]

With the reorganization in 1982, 19th Infantry Brigade at Colchester was assigned to 3rd Armoured Division in Germany. On 1 Apr 1986 it transferred to 4th Armoured Division. 24th Infantry Brigade, as noted, had a BAOR reinforcement role. Originally, infantry battalions in the UK were simply "leg" units, as all mechanised battalions were located in Germany. However, after introduction of the Saxon wheeled APC beginning in late 1983, battalions in the UK with a BAOR reinforcement role began to be mechanised in the new APC.

In 1960, NATO's Allied Command Europe (ACE) established a Mobile Force. This was to be a small collection of units (air and ground) which could be

---

[198] Volunteer battalions were cut to three rifle companies following Options for Change, losing their heavy weapons. However, four battalions were converted as fire support battalions, with two companies each (each company had GPMG, 81mm mortar, and Milan ATGM platoons). These companies (eight in all) were intended to support battalions with a BAOR reinforcement role. Hence the inference that eight battalions may have been intended for such purposes earlier.

[199] The brigade was reorganized (by ca. 1986) with a Saxon-mounted infantry battalion and two light battalions with additional ATGW that could be carried in RAF helicopters. The idea was that it would serve as a rear-area tank-killing force.

[200] In Apr 1993 it would relocated to Colchester and be reorganized with two infantry battalions and two regiments AAC. It was tasked from 1992 to become part of Multinational Division Central (Airmobile) [MND(C)], which was formally activated Apr 1994. 24th Airmobile Brigade was replaced by 16th Air Assault Brigade in Sep 1999. No longer having a clear role, MND(C) was closed down in Oct 2002.

assembled if necessary and sent on short notice to any part of the Allied
Command Europe's territory. In practice, it was intended for operations on the
periphery (e.g., to Norway or to Turkey) since a few light battalions would be
irrelevant in Germany. The land element was known as ACE Mobile Force
(Land): AMF(L) or AMFL. The British contribution was a reinforced infantry
battalion (generally one based at Dover); 249 Signal Squadron was formed at
Old Sarum in 1972 to support AMFL.[201] Overall, AMFL would be brigade-
strength (around 6000); while the force conducted periodic exercises in Europe,
it had the disadvantage of being an ad hoc formation.

In Apr 1994, NATO created the Multi National Division (Central)
[MND(C)]was also known as the Multi National Airmobile Division. It was
one of two multi national divisions created under the Allied Command Europe
Rapid Reaction Corps (ARRC). It had a division headquarters (at
Rheindahlen), and its main forces were four brigades from four different
nations,[202] along with various divisional troops. The 24th Airmobile Brigade
was assigned to the new division. When that brigade went out of existence in
Sep 1999, the new 16th Air Assault Brigade joined in its place. Great Britain
also provided an air defense regiment and other artillery support (observation
post battery and an artillery surveillance, recce and target acquisition unit). The
division ceased to have a liability for operations in Jul 2002, and officially
closed down 25 Oct 2002.

Multi-National Division
(Central)

---

[201] In a 1998 exercise, the British contribution was about 1450 strong and included an
infantry battalion, armoured squadron, surveillance and target acquisition battery,
artillery battery, signals squadron, engineer field troop, AAC flight, transport squadron,
ordnance company, REME workshop, and medical detachment.
[202] In addition to the British component, the division included the Belgian Para-
Commando Brigade, Dutch 11 Airmobile Brigade, and German 31 Airlanding Brigade.

Berlin 1948—1994

The troops in Berlin were always separate from BAOR. From Nov 1946 the garrison there comprised a detached armoured squadron and two infantry battalions. This was expanded Feb 1948 to three battalions. The total force was known as British Troops Berlin; there was no distinct brigade headquarters. In Feb 1949 the force was redesignated as Area Troops Berlin. Berlin Independent Brigade was established in Oct 1953. It was redesignated Apr 1959 as Berlin Infantry Brigade Group and Dec 1963 as Berlin Infantry Brigade. In Apr 1977 it became Berlin Field Force; in Jan 1981 it resumed the title of Berlin Infantry Brigade.

The normal garrison from the 1960s was an armoured squadron and three infantry battalions; by 1986 a detached air defence troop was assigned. The brigade numbered around 3100 personnel. Berlin Infantry Brigade was reduced from 1992: as battalions completed their tours they were not replaced. Thus the brigade went to two battalions in 1992 and one in 1993. It was disbanded in Sep 1994.

In 1958, 38 (Berlin) Field Squadron RE joined the garrison. In 1959, the Berlin Brigade Signal Squadron became 229 Signal Squadron. This squadron was enlarged to 29 HQ & Signal Regiment in Jan 1988 and reverted to 229 Signal Squadron in Jan 1993. 7th Flight AAC joined in Jun 1977.

Between 1948 and 1952, the armoured squadron was provided from regiments in Germany :

Feb 1948	Sqn, 11 Hussars [armoured cars]
May 1949	'A' Sqn, Royal Dragoons [armoured cars]
Mar 1950	'A' Sqn, Royal Horse Guards [armoured cars]
Feb 1951	Sqn, 3rd Hussars

In Feb 1952 a permanent unit was formed, designated 1st Independent Sqn Royal Tank Regt. It was disbanded Dec 1957.

Between Dec 1957 and Aug 1963, the squadron came from the APC regiment in BAOR:

Dec 1957	'B' Sqn, 14th/20th Hussars
Nov 1960	'C' Sqn, 4th Royal Tank Regt

Another permanent unit was established in Mar 1963, designated Independent Sqn Royal Tank Regt; it was disbanded Nov 1965.

After that date, the squadron normally came from the training regiment at Catterick:

Feb 1965	Sqn, Queens Own Hussars
Feb 1967	Sqn, 1st Royal Tank Regt
Jan 1969	Sqn, 9th/12th Lancers
Dec 1970	Sqn, 1st Queen's DG
Dec 1972	'A' Sqn, 4th Royal Tank Regt
Dec 1974	'B' Sqn, 5th Royal Inniskilling DG
Dec 1976	'B' Sqn, Royal Scots DG
Apr 1979	'D' Sqn, Royal Hussars
Feb 1981	'D' Sqn, 4th/7th DG
Apr 1983	'D' Sqn, Queens Own Hussars
May 1985	'B' Sqn, 14th/20th Hussars

From 1987, the squadron came from the 14th/20th Hussars at Munster:

Dec 1987	'D' Sqn
Sep 1988	'C' Sqn

The squadron was withdrawn in 1991.

The three infantry battalions were:

1st Bn Royal Norfolk Regiment [assigned Jan 1948]
      replaced May 1949- 1st Bn Royal Welch Fusiliers
      replaced Sep 1950- 1st Bn Manchester Regt
      replaced Apr 1951- 1st Bn Durham LI
      replaced May 1952- 1st Bn Royal Scots
      replaced Jul 1953- 1st Bn KO Yorkshire LI
      replaced Sep 1954- 1st Bn Manchester Regt
      replaced Jan 1956- 1st Bn Black Watch
      replaced Dec 1957-1st Bn Border Regt
      replaced Jul 1959-1st Bn Y & L Regt
      replaced Dec 1960-1st Bn 2nd Green Jackets
      replaced Jul 1962-1st Bn Kings Regiment
      replaced Jul 1964-1st Bn 3rd East Anglian Regt [redesignated 3rd
          Bn Royal Anglian Regt]
      replaced Aug 1966-1st Bn Queens Own Highlanders
      replaced Sep 1968- 1st Bn Staffordshire Regt
      replaced Nov 1970-1st Bn Cheshire Regt
      replaced Dec 1972-1st Bn Coldstream Guards
      replaced Jan 1975- 3rd Bn Royal Green Jackets
      replaced Jan 1977- 1st Bn Welsh Guards
      replaced Jul 1979- 1st Bn Grenadier Guards
      replaced Dec 1981- 2nd Bn Royal Irish Rangers

replaced Dec 1983- 1st Bn Royal Hampshire Regt
replaced Feb 1986- 1st Bn Gloucestershire Regt
replaced Feb 1988- 1st Bn Kings Regiment
replaced Jan 1990- 1st Bn Irish Guards
replaced Mar 1992- 1st Bn Queens Lancashire Regt [withdrawn
    Aug 1994]

2nd Bn Royal Scots Fusiliers [assigned Feb 1948]
    replaced Feb 1949-2nd Bn Queens Royal Regt
      [redesignated 1949 as 1st Bn of regiment]
    replaced Dec 1949- 1st Bn Royal Fusiliers
    replaced Feb 1951- 1st Bn Kings Liverpool Regt
    replaced Jun 1952- 1st Bn Welsh Guards
    replaced Jul 1953- 1st Bn Royal Irish Fusiliers
    replaced Jun 1954- 1st Bn Royal Lincolnshire Regt
    replaced May 1955- 1st Bn Cheshire Regt
    replaced Jan 1957- 1st Bn South Lancashire Regt
    replaced Jan 1958- 1st Bn Royal Inniskilling Fusiliers
    replaced Feb 1959- 1st Bn Kings Own Scottish Borderers
    replaced Apr 1961- 1st Bn Welch Regt
    replaced Oct 1963- 1st Bn Somerset &Cornwall LI
    replaced Oct 1965- 1st Bn Royal Inniskilling Fusiliers
    replaced Oct 1967- 1st Bn Gloucestershire Regt
    replaced Oct 1969- 2nd Bn Royal Regt of Fusiliers
    replaced Jul 1971- 1st Bn DERR
    replaced May 1973- 1st Bn KOSB
    replaced May 1975- 1st Bn Royal Regt of Wales
    replaced May 1977- 2nd Bn Parachute Regt
    replaced Jun 1979- 1st Bn Royal Irish Rangers
    replaced Apr 1981- 2nd Bn Royal Regt of Fusiliers
    replaced Jun 1983- 1st Bn POWY
    replaced Apr 1985- 1st Bn Devon & Dorset Regt
    replaced Feb 1987- 1st Bn KOSB
    replaced Jan 1989- 1st Bn Light Infantry
    replaced Jun 1991- 1st Bn Gordon Highlanders [withdrawn Aug
      1993]

1st Bn Worcestershire Regiment [assigned Feb 1948]
    replaced May 1949-1st Bn Gordon Highlanders
    replaced Sep 1950- 1st Bn Black Watch
    replaced Nov 1951- 1st Bn East Yorkshire Regt
    replaced Jul 1953- 1st Bn Royal Scots Fusiliers
    replaced Mar 1954- 1st Bn Grenadier Guards

replaced Mar 1955- 1st Bn A & S Highlanders
replaced Jul 1956- 1st Bn Royal Welch Fusiliers
replaced Feb 1958- 1st Bn Royal Scots
replaced Feb 1960- 1st Bn 2nd East Anglian Regt
replaced Jul 1961- 1st Bn Durham LI
replaced Jun 1963- 1st Bn POWY
replaced Apr 1965- 1st Bn 1st Green Jackets [redesignated 1st
        Bn RGJ]
replaced Apr 1967- 1st Bn KOYLI [redesignated 2nd Bn LI]
replaced Apr 1969- 1st Bn A & S Highlanders
replaced Jul 1970- 1st Queens Regt
replaced Jul 1972- 1st Bn W&SFR
replaced Aug 1974- 1st Bn Parachute Regt
replaced Aug 1976- 1st Bn Green Howards
replaced Aug 1978- 2nd Bn Royal Anglian Regt
replaced Jan 1981- 1st Bn KORB Regt
replaced Mar 1983- 3rd Bn Royal Regt of Fusiliers
replaced Mar 1985- 1st Bn Royal Highland Fusiliers
replaced Mar 1987- 1st Bn Black Watch
replaced Jul 1989- 1st Bn Royal Welch Fusiliers [withdrawn Jul
        1992]

Exit BAOR

With the apparent success of the [first] Gulf War and then the end of the Cold War, the British Army suffered "Options for Change" which greatly reduced its strength. 1 Corps was disbanded 1 Oct 1992, and became the nucleus for the Allied Command Europe Rapid Reaction Corps (ARRC). The various divisions and brigades in Germany were disbanded or shuffled. 1st Armoured Division was disbanded 31 Dec 1992 (with its HQ surviving briefly as HQ Lower Saxony District). However, it was then reformed 1 Jul 1993 in Germany as 1st (UK) Armoured Division, by redesignation of 4th Armoured Division. The new division had its HQ located at Herford, with 4th Armoured Brigade (Osnabrück), 7th Armoured Brigade (Bergen-Hohne), and 20th Armoured Brigade (Paderborn). 3rd Armoured Division relocated to Bulford, UK, in Sep 1992, where it became 3rd (UK) Division and the only other tactical division in the Army.[203] 4th Armoured Division disappeared, as noted, to reform 1st Armoured Division. BAOR itself was disbanded 31 Mar 1994. Details of these changes were largely contained in the 1990—1994 orbat above, at page 113.

Following the amalgamations in 1992-93 under "Options for Change" there were only eight tank regiments in the Army, with the last one converting to Challenger 1 in 1994. (Six regiments would remain in Germany and the other two would be in the UK.) By this stage each regiment had been reduced to three squadrons, with a total fleet of 24 squadrons. (A regiment would have 38 tanks.) Under the Strategic Defense Review, the Army ended up with six regiments of four squadrons each, all of which were to receive the Challenger 2. A regiment would then have 56 or 58 tanks. But, since the introduction of Whole Fleet Management in 1999, each regiment has only 30 tanks on strength—shared among the squadrons as needed—and the rest of the Challenger 2 fleet is kept in storage at the Base Vehicle Depot in UK to be issued as and when required by operations. (This has led to a considerable reduction in REME 2nd line servicing units).

The locating regiment, withdrawn to the UK in 1985, was placed in suspended animation 4 Sep 1993.

---

[203] It thus took over the reinforcement role for Germany, taking over the 1st and 19th Mechanised Brigades and 5th Airborne Brigade. However, both it and the Germany-based 1st (UK) Armoured Division were heavily tasked throughout the 1990s providing forces for the Balkans because of problems in the former Yugoslavia.

Army troops in Germany not part of 1st (UK) Armoured Division came under the new UK Support Command (Germany), which was established in 1994 with its headquarters at Rheindahlen. It adopted BAOR's formation sign. In 1999, most of its responsibilities transferred to the new 102nd Logistic Brigade. 1st (UK) Armoured Division had two armoured regiments and two armoured infantry battalions in each of its brigades, along with an armoured recce regiment as divisional troops. Its Division Artillery Group (DAG) was organized with three regiments of SP 155mm howitzers and a light air defence regiment with Starstreak HVM SAMs. In wartime it would also have a regiment with the 227mm MLRS; in peacetime that unit remains based in the UK. The division also has a regiment of the Army Air Corps; four regiments of engineers;[204] four regiments of the Royal Logistics Corps; three battalions REME; and other support units. In 1998, under the Strategic Defence Review, the government announced that the three armoured brigades would each lose an armoured regiment, and this was undertaken beginning in Jul 1999 as regiments rotated out of Germany. In addition, the artillery regiments each lost a battery.[205]

The Apr 1996 strength of British Army forces in Germany was 16,700 in 1st (UK) Armoured Division and 4,100 in UKSC(G). A number of the support units in the latter were moved under the division, which grew to 17,200 while UKSC(G) shrank to 800 personnel (circa 1999). 102nd Logistic Brigade HQ was established in Germany in Jul 1999, taking over some RLC units in Germany along with other support units stationed in the UK.[206] The current nominal strength of 1st (UK) Armoured Division is 16,800 and that of UKSC(G) is 600. The latter may include 102 Logistic Brigade in its total.

Not all of the brigades were retained at the same operational readiness. Under the BOWMAN scheme, from 1999 brigades proceeded through a three year cycle: Year 1- training, Year 2- fully operational and deployed if required, and Year 3- lower order of readiness but can be deployed as back up. This system applied both to the armoured brigades of 1st (UK) Armoured Division in Germany and the mechanised brigades of 3rd (UK) Division in the UK. For the 2001-2 period, it appeared that 20th Armoured Brigade (Paderborn) was in the Year 1 (training) phase; 4th Armoured Brigade (Osnabrück) was in year 2

---

[204] One regiment provided GS for Germany and the other three were allotted for CS of the three armoured brigades. The three CS regiments were all reorganized around 1999 to comprise three armoured engineer squadrons in place of the former field squadrons.
[205] In theory, in the case of war each would receive a fourth battery from the UK.
[206] Combat Service Support Group (Germany) [CSSG(G)] was formed Jan 1993 to provide third-line logistic support to the maneuver units. Its HQ was retitled Jul 1999 as HQ 102 Logistic Brigade.

(deployable), and 7th Armoured Brigade (Hohne) was in the Year 3 (back-up) phase.

3rd (UK) Division was the only other significant formation left in the British Army. It was tasked both for national contingencies and the ARRC, and it shared the burden of providing units for the Balkans. With headquarters at Bulford, it initially had 1st and 19th Mechanised Brigades (Bulford and Catterick) and 5th Airborne Brigade (Aldershot). 24th Airmobile Brigade (Catterick) was the only other field formation in the Army. In Sep 1999 5th Airborne Brigade was reorganized into 12th Mechanised Brigade. Many of its units then went to help form the new 16th Air Assault Brigade. That brigade was formed at Catterick, taking over the helicopter units and other portions of the disbanded 24th Airmobile Brigade.

1st (UK) Armoured Division was tasked for command of the British ground forces in Operation TELIC, the UK contribution to the 2003 invasion of Iraq, or second Gulf War. Forces were deployed to the Gulf area from Jan to Mar 2003, and the invasion began 20 Mar 2003. Ground troops were drawn from both Germany and the UK. Those from Germany included HQ and 207 Signal Squadron, 7th Armoured Brigade, along with its two tank and two mechanised infantry battalions. These were supplemented by elements from the two other brigades in Germany. Artillery and engineers were drawn from a number of units in Germany. (16th Air Assault Brigade from the UK was the other major British ground unit, exclusive of the Royal Marines' 3rd Commando Brigade.) 102nd Logistical Brigade from Germany was the major command element for supporting units. The invasion was declared a success by the US president 1 May 2003, although troops remained in Iraq on occupation duties.

1st (UK) Armoured Division was relieved by 3rd (UK) Division 11 Jul 2003 and returned to Germany. By that point, both the 7th Armoured and 16th Air Assault Brigades were redeployed to home stations, with the UK-based 19th Mechanised Brigade taking over security duties. (101st Logistic Brigade from the UK replaced 102nd Logistic Brigade as well.) 19th Mechanised Brigade was replaced Nov 2003 by Germany-based 20th Armoured Brigade, and they were in turn replaced by the UK-based 1st Mechanised Brigade in Apr 2004.[207] From Jul 2003 onwards, units deployed were both Germany- and UK-based, regardless of the source of the brigade headquarters.

---

[207] When 3rd (UK) Division was due for replacement in Apr 2004, the Army created a composite headquarters for Multinational Division (South-East), drawing mainly on Germany-based 16th Signal Regiment for communications. Thus, 1st (UK) Armoured Division Headquarters and Signal Regiment did not have to return to Iraq. MD(SE) controlled troops from other nations as well as the British brigade.

The key point here is that there is no longer any clear delineation of operational roles between British troops in Germany or those in the UK. This may change under the Future Army Structure (FAS) announced in 2004. Some key points include the re-roling of 4th Armoured Brigade (Germany) to mechanised and 19th Mechanised Brigade (UK) to light. The number of tank squadrons will be cut, although each armoured or mechanised brigade is to have its own reconnaissance regiment. Changes to the infantry will include fixing individual battalions by role, ending the current policy of re-roling (e.g., from light infantry to mechanised or armoured infantry) on changes of station. Changes will affect the other arms and services as well, along with the Territorial Army.

Details of the forces in Germany from 1994 are contained on the next page.

☐ *Forces in Germany From 1994*

Some units from BAOR lingered in Germany into 1995 before disbanding or relocating to the UK. These are listed at the end of this section, which is intended to show the final organization of British Army forces in Germany. Various units from Germany have served in the Balkans during this time. This included division and brigade headquarters along with various combat, combat support, and combat service support troops. No attempt is made here to detail that service. The Army in Germany were also tapped for contributions to the second Gulf War (Operation TELIC) beginning in 2003; an assignment that still (early 2005) continues.[208]

1st (UK) Armoured Division

1st Armoured Division HQ & Signal Regt[209]   *Herford*
     208th, 211th, 212th Signal Sqns

The Light Dragoons [recce]   *Hohne*
     replaced Aug 2000 by 9th/12th Royal Lancers
     replaced Sep 2003 by 1st Queen's Dragoon Guards[210]

Division Artillery Group[211]
4th Regt RA   *Osnabrück*
     3/29, 52,[212] 88, 97 Field Btys RA [AS90], 94 HQ Bty RA

---

[208] Details of service are given for the initial operation, along with the 2nd, 3rd and 4th roulements (Operations TELIC, TELIC 2, TELIC 3 and TELIC 4), covering the period through mid 2004.

[209] Sent to Kuwait for the Mar 2003 invasion of Iraq; GOC 1st (UK) Armoured Division was also GOC British Land Forces in the Gulf. Following the initial operations, division HQ was the command element for Multinational Division (South-East) until it was replaced 11 Jul 2003 by 3rd (UK) Division.

[210] Sent to the Gulf under 1st (UK) Armoured Division for Operation TELIC.

[211] Under the Strategic Defense Review, the three field regiments were to reduce from four to three gun batteries in peacetime, with a fourth battery to return during wartime. The division would be reinforced in wartime by an MLRS-equipped regiment from the UK.

[212] 52 Field Bty RA withdrawn from the regiment Nov 2000. It remained in Germany until Sep 2003 as part of the UK-based 19 Regt RA.

26th Regt RA[213]   *Gütersloh*
    16, 17, 127,[214] 159 Field Btys RA [AS90], 55 HQ Bty RA
40th Regt RA   *Hohne*
    6/36, 38, 129, 137[215] Field Btys RA [AS90], 49 HQ Bty RA
    replaced Jul 1998 by 3rd Regiment RHA[216] {C, D, J, N[217] Btys RHA
        [AS90], M HQ Bty RHA}
12th Regt RA   *Dortmund*; Aug 1995 to *Sennelager*
    9, 12, 58 AD Btys RA, T HQ Bty RA[218]
16th Regt RA   *Paderborn* [left Oct 1995]
    14, 30, 32 AD Btys RA [Rapier]

21 Engineer Regt[219]   *Nienburg*; moved 1996 to *Osnabrück*
    1, 4 Field Sqns RE, 45 Sp Sqn RE, 7 HQ Sqn RE
    reorganized from 1999 with 1, 4 and new (operational 2001) 73 Armd
    Engr Sqns RE and 7 HQ Sqn RE
28 Engineer Regt[220]   *Hameln*
    23 Amphib Sqn RE, 64 HQ Sqn RE, 65 Field Pk Sqn RE, 412 Trp RE
    Dec 1999 added 42 Field Sqn RE and 45 Sp Sqn RE; 65 reorganized
    as Field Sp Sqn RE
32 Engineer Regt[221]   *Hohne*
    26, 31, 77 Field Sqns RE, 2 HQ Sqn RE
    reorganized 1999 with 26, 31 and 39 Armd Engr Sqns RE and 1 HQ
    Sqn RE

---

[213] May have been at Paderborn and then moved to Gütersloh during this period. Elements of the regiment joined 3rd Regt RHA for Operation TELIC in 2003. The regiment served in Operation TELIC 3 under 4th Armoured Brigade.

[214] 127 Field Bty RA withdrawn from the regiment Nov 2000. It remained in Germany until Sep 2003 as part of the UK-based 19 Regt RA.

[215] 137 Field Bty RA reduced to cadre in 1997.

[216] Sent to the Gulf under 7th Armoured Brigade for Operation TELIC.

[217] N Bty RHA left the regiment Nov 1999.

[218] Originally Rapier and HVM; by 1998 all HVM.

[219] Allotted for CS of 4th Armoured Brigade.

[220] This regiment has a GS role in Germany. Sent to the Gulf under 1st (UK) Armoured Division for Operation TELIC, where it was in control of its own 23 Amphib Sqn RE along with 45 Sp Sqn RE from 21 Regiment, 29 Armoured Engr Sqn from 35 Regiment and 70 Gurkha Field Sqn RE from 36 Regiment (UK). 42 Field Sqn RE was transferred to the regiment Dec 1999.

[221] Allotted for CS of 7th Armoured Brigade. Sent to the Gulf under 7th Armoured Brigade for Operation TELIC, adding 25 Armoured Engr Sqn from 38 Regiment (UK).

35 Engineer Regt[222]   *Hameln*; moved Dec 1999 to *Paderborn*[223]
    29, 37, 42 Field Sqns RE, 44 HQ Sqn RE
    reorganized 1999 with 29, 37 and 77 Armd Engr Sqns RE and 44 HQ
    Sqn RE

1st Regt Army Air Corps   *Gütersloh*
    651st, 652nd, 661st Sqns AAC[224]

1st Regiment Royal Military Police[225]   *Herford*
    110 Provost Coy   *Gütersloh*
    111 Provost Coy   *Hohne*
    115 Provost Coy   *Osnabrück*

1st General Support Regt RLC[226]   Gütersloh
    2, 12, 22, 43 Sqns RLC, 98 PC Sqn RLC, 74 HQ Sqn RLC
2nd Close Support Regt RLC[227]   Gütersloh
    11, 23, 45, 76 Sqns RLC, 27 HQ Sqn RLC

1st Bn REME   Osnabrück
2nd Bn REME[228]   Hohne
3rd Bn REME   Paderborn

1st Armoured Field Ambulance   Hohne
2nd Armoured Field Ambulance   Osnabrück
3rd Armoured Field Ambulance   Paderborn

---

[222] Allotted for CS of 20th Armoured Brigade. The regiment served in Operation TELIC 3 under 4th Armoured Brigade, with its own 37 and 77 Armoured Engr Sqns, 15 Sp Sqn—replaced by 45 Sp Sqn (21 Regiment), and 100 Field Sqn RE (Militia) (Royal Monmouthshire Royal Engineers).

[223] The move to Paderborn actually occurred from Dec 1999 to May 2000.

[224] Each currently equipped with 8 Lynx attack helicopters. 651st Sqn AAC moved to the UK in 2002.

[225] The division originally had a provost company; 1st Regiment Royal Military Police was formed 1 Apr 1996. The regiment was sent to the Gulf under 1st (UK) Armoured Division for Operation TELIC. Elements of the regiment returned to Iraq for Operation TELIC 3.

[226] Sent to the Gulf under 1st (UK) Armoured Division for Operation TELIC. 2 and 12 are transport squadrons, 22 Transport Sqn RLC was added 2001; 43 is a support squadron; 98 is a postal and courier squadron.

[227] Sent to the Gulf under 1st (UK) Armoured Division for Operation TELIC . 11, 23 and 76 are brigade support squadrons (support of 4th, 20th and 7th Armoured Brigades, respectively) and 45 is a division support squadron.

[228] Sent to the Gulf under 1st (UK) Armoured Division for Operation TELIC.

[The three armoured field ambulances merged as 1st CS Medical Regt in 2000, with RHQ at Munster, two squadrons at Munster and one at Hohne.][229]

 4th Armoured Brigade[230]

HQ & 204th Signal Sqn   *Osnabrück*
Kings Royal Hussars   *Munster*
  replaced Feb 2000 by Royal Dragoon Guards
Queens Royal Lancers[231]   *Osnabrück* [left Aug 2003 w/o replacement]
1st Bn Coldstream Guards   *Munster*
  replaced Feb 1998 by 1st Bn Irish Guards[232]
  replaced Oct 2003 by 1st Bn Scots Guards
1st Bn Green Howards   *Osnabrück*
  replaced Feb 2000 by 1st Bn Duke of Wellington's Regt[233]

 7th Armoured Brigade[234]

207 HQ & 207th Signal Sqn[235]   *Hohne*
Queen's Royal Hussars   *Hohne*
  replaced 1996 by Royal Scots Dgn Gds[236] at *Fallingbostel*
2nd Royal Tank Regt[237]   *Hohne*

---

[229] 1st Close Support Medical Regt sent to the Gulf under 1st (UK) Armoured Division for Operation TELIC.

[230] Infantry battalions for 4th Armoured Brigade come from The Guards Division and The King's Division.

[231] Some elements from unit sent to the Gulf for Operation TELIC to reinforce units assigned to 7th Armoured Brigade.

[232] Some elements from unit sent to the Gulf for Operation TELIC to reinforce units assigned to 7th Armoured Brigade.

[233] Sent to the Gulf for Operation TELIC as supplemental infantry under 1st (UK) Armoured Division.

[234] Infantry battalions for 7th Armoured Brigade come from The Scottish Division and The Queen's Division.

[235] Sent to the Gulf under 1st (UK) Armoured Division for Operation TELIC.

[236] Sent to the Gulf under 7th Armoured Brigade for Operation TELIC.

[237] Sent to the Gulf under 7th Armoured Brigade for Operation TELIC. Elements of the regiment remained for Operation TELIC 2 (Jul-Nov 2003). To move to Tidworth in 2005 without replacement.

[7th Armoured Brigade]
1st Bn Royal Highland Fusiliers   *Hohne*
     replaced Jun 2000 by 1st Bn Black Watch[238]   replaced Mar 2004 by
1st Bn Highlanders
2nd Bn Royal Anglian Regt   *Celle*
     replaced Feb 1996 by 2nd Bn Royal Regt of Fusiliers
     replaced May 2001 by 1st Bn Royal Regt of Fusiliers[239]

 20th Armoured Brigade[240]

HQ & 200th Signal Sqn[241]   *Paderborn*; moved 1999 to *Sennelager*
1st The Queen's Dragoon Guards   *Sennelager*
     replaced Aug 1998[242] by Queen's Royal Hussars[243]
Royal Dragoon Guards   *Paderborn*
     replaced Jun 1996 by 1st Royal Tank Regt [left Jun 1999 w/o
          replacement]
1st Bn Devonshire & Dorset Regt   *Paderborn*
     replaced Jan 1998 by1st Bn Royal Regt of Wales[244]
2nd Bn Light Infantry   *Paderborn*
     replaced Jan 1997 by 2nd Bn Royal Green Jackets
     replaced Apr 2002 by 1st Bn Light Infantry[245]

---

[238] Sent to the Gulf under 7th Armoured Brigade for Operation TELIC.

[239] Sent to the Gulf under 7th Armoured Brigade for Operation TELIC.

[240] Infantry Battalions for 20th Armoured Brigade come from The Prince of Wales's Division and The Light Division.

[241] Deployed to Iraq as the main component of Operation TELIC 3 (Nov 2003—Apr 2004). Some battalions from other sources were assigned to the brigade.

[242] However, 1st QDG may have left Germany as early as Jan 1998.

[243] Served in Operation TELIC 3 under 4th Armoured Brigade.

[244] Served in Operation TELIC 3 under 4th Armoured Brigade.

[245] Some elements from unit sent to the Gulf for Operation TELIC to reinforce units assigned to 7th Armoured Brigade. The battalion served in Operation TELIC 3 under 4th Armoured Brigade.

Other Forces in Germany

1st (UK) Signal Brigade[246]	*Rheindahlen*
7th (ARRC) Signal Regt	*Krefeld*; moved 2002 to *Elmpt*
229th, 231st, 232nd Signal Sqns	
16th Signal Regt[247]	*Rheindahlen*; moved 2002 to *Elmpt*
230th, 252nd, 253rd, 255th Signal Sqns[248]	
Support Bn HQ ARRC[249]	*Rheindahlen*
14th Topographic Sqn RE[250]	*Mönchen-Gladbach*

UK Support Command (Germany)
[This currently appears to be only a small group with responsibility for the garrisons in Germany. It probably also controls the following RLC units: 30th Coach Sqn and 69th Movement Control Sqn. Most of its original units and duties were taken over by 102nd Logistic Brigade.]

---

[246] Command element for the 7th and 16th Signal Regts and Support Bn. Established 1 Apr 1995, initially to command signal units in the former Yugoslavia. 14th (EW) Signal Regt has also been under the brigade's command.

[247] Deployed to Iraq Apr 2004 for Operation TELIC 4, in support of HQ Multinational Division (South-East).

[248] 230th Signal Sqn transferred to 7th Signal Regt 1994 and returned 1997. 253rd Signal Sqn reduced to a troop in 1996 and placed under 252nd Signal Sqn.

[249] Provides life support, administration, and logistic support to HQ ARRC, both in peace and on operations. Also responsible for defence and security of the command post in wartime.

[250] Sent to the Gulf under 1st (UK) Armoured Division for Operation TELIC. Later redesignated 14 Geographic Sqn RE. This unit comes under 42 Engineer Regt (Geographic) in the UK.

102ND LOGISTIC BRIGADE [formed Jul 1999][251]

HQ 102nd Logistic Brigade[252]	*Gütersloh*[253]

6th Supply Regiment RLC[254]

600th HQ Sqn RLC	*Gütersloh*
61st Ammunition Sqn RLC	*Gütersloh*
62nd Stores Sqn RLC	*Gütersloh*
67th Supply Services Sqn RLC	*Dulmen*
68th Log Bde Sp Sqn RLC	*Dulmen*

7th Transport Regiment RLC[255]

617th HQ Sqn RLC	*Bielefeld*
9th Fuel Sp Sqn RLC	*Bielefeld*
16th Tank Transporter Sqn RLC	*Fallingbostel*
17th Transport Sqn RLC	*Bielefeld*

8th Transport Regiment RLC[256]

5th HQ Sqn RLC	*Catterick, UK*
3rd Tank Transporter Sqn RLC	*Catterick, UK*
13th Transport Sqn RLC	*Catterick, UK*
29th Transport Sqn RLC	*Catterick, UK*
64th Fuel Sp Sqn RLC	*Gütersloh*[257]

5th Regiment RMP (Vol)[258]

Regiment HQ	*Edinburgh, UK*
101st Provost Co RMP	*Düsseldorf*
243rd Provost Co RMP (Vol)	*Livingston, UK*
252nd Provost Co RMP (Vol)	*Stockton-On-Tees, UK*

---

[251] From 1 Apr 2001 the brigade was placed operationally under UKLF, as is 1st (UK) Armoured Division. It is currently subordinated to HQ Theatre Troops in Netheravon.

[252] Sent to the Gulf for Operation TELIC, serving as the National Support Element for British Armed Forces in the theater. All of the assigned units shown except 8th Transport Regt RLC went with it, and it was strengthened by a number of other units from the UK.

[253] Brigadier also serves as commander of Gütersloh Garrison.

[254] Added two squadrons at Dulmen from 14th Supply Regt RLC in 1998.

[255] Formed in 1993 from elements 7 Tank Transporter and 10 Corps Transport Regts RCT.

[256] The regiment moved from Germany to the UK in 1994. Deployed to Iraq Apr 2004 for Operation TELIC 4.

[257] Transferred Dec 2003 from 6th Supply Regt RLC to 8th Transport Regt RLC.

[258] Formed 1 Apr 2000.

[102nd Logistic Brigade]

334th Field Hospital	*Edinburgh, UK*
102 Mil Working Dog Sp Unit RAVC	*Sennelager*
262nd Signal Sqn	*Gütersloh*

Lingering Units

The following remained in Germany after 1994, although not forming part of the new structure:

5th Heavy Regt RA at Hildesheim [to UK 1995]
39th Heavy Regt RA at Sennelager [to UK Aug 1995]
16th Air Defence Regt RA at Dortmund [to UK Aug 1995]

4th Regt AAC at Detmold [to UK Mar 1995]

14th Signal Regt (EW) at Celle [to UK Jan 1996]

Commanders In Chief BAOR And General Officers Commanding 1 Corps[259]

Commanders in Chief, BAOR

Aug 1945	F.M. The Rt Hon Bernard Law (Montgomery), 1st Viscount Montgomery of Alamein, KG, GCB, DSO
Jun 1946	Lt-Gen. Sir Richard Loudon McCreery, GCB, KBE, DSO, MC
Nov 1947	Lt-Gen. Sir Brian Herbert Robertson, Bt., GCB, KCMG, KCVO, DSO, MC, ADC
Sep 1949	Lt-Gen. Sir Charles Frederic Keightley, GCB, KBE, DSO, ADC
Aug 1951	Lt-Gen. Sir Allan Francis John Harding, GCB, CBE, DSO, MC
24 Sep 1952	Gen. Sir Richard Nelson Gale, GCB, KBE, DSO, MC
1 Jan 1957	Gen. Sir Dudley Ward, GCB, KBE, DSO
Jan 1960	Gen. Sir Archibald James Halkett Cassels, GCB, KBE, DSO
1 Apr 1963	Gen. Sir William Gurdon Stirling, GCB, CBE, DSO
Apr 1966	Gen. Sir John Winthrop Hackett, GCB, CBE, DSO, MC
10 Jul 1968	Gen. Sir Geoffrey Richard Desmond Fitzpatrick, KCB, DSO, MBE, MC
Sep 1970	Gen. Sir Peter Mervyn Hunt, KCB, DSO, OBE
Apr 1973	Gen. Sir Harry Tuzo, GCB, OBE, MC
Jan 1976	Gen. Sir Frank King, GCB, MBE
30 Sep 1978	Gen. Sir William Norman Roy Scotter, KCB, OBE, MC
25 Oct 1980	Gen. Sir James Michael Gow, KCB, ADC
1 Jul 1983	Gen. Sir Nigel Thomas Bagnall, GCB, CVO, MC
1 Jul 1985	Gen. Sir Martin Farndale, KCB
Nov 1987	Gen. Brian Leslie Graham Kenny
26 Nov 1989	Gen. Sir Peter Anthony Inge, GCB
31 Jul 1993	Gen. Sir Charles Ronald Llewelyn Guthrie, GCB, LVO, OBE, ADC
Mar 1994	BAOR disbanded and position abolished

---

[259] Details in this section are mainly from the following pages of T. F. Mills' exceptional web site: http://regiments.org/formations/uk-cmdarmy/os-baor.htm (BAOR), http://regiments.org/formations/uk-corps/corps1.htm (1 Corps), http://regiments.org/formations/uk-corps/corpsarrc.htm (ARRC).

General Officers Commanding 1 (BR) Corps

Nov 1951	Lt-Gen. Sir Dudley Ward, GCB, KBE, DSO
Jan 1953	Lt-Gen. Sir (Archibald) James Halkett Cassels, GCB, KBE, DSO
Apr 1954	Lt-Gen. Sir Hugh Charles Stockwell, GCB, KBE, DSO[260]
Dec 1956	Lt-Gen. Sir Harold E. Pyman, GBE, KCB, DSO
Mar 1958	Lt-Gen. Michael West
Jan 1960	Lt-Gen. Charles Jones
Mar 1962	Lt-Gen. Kenneth Darling
Dec 1963	Lt-Gen. Richard Goodwin
Jan 1966	Lt-Gen. John Mogg
Jan 1967	Lt-Gen. Mervyn Butler
Jan 1970	Lt-Gen. John Sharp
14 Jan 1972	Lt-Gen. Sir Roland Christopher Gibbs, KCB, CBE, DSO, MC
24 Jan 1974	Lt-Gen. Sir Jack W. Harman, KCB, OBE, MC
5 Apr 1976	Lt-Gen. Sir Richard Edward Worsley, KCB, OBE
22 Jul 1978	Lt-Gen. Sir Peter John Hall Leng, KCB, MBE, MC
Oct 1980	Lt-Gen. Sir Nigel Thomas Bagnall, KCB, CVO, MC
May 1983	Lt-Gen. Sir Martin Baker Farndale, KCB
May 1985	Lt-Gen. Sir Brian Leslie Graham Kenny, KCB, CBE
8 Aug 1987	Lt-Gen. Sir Peter Anthony Inge, KG, GCB
30 Sep 1989	Lt-Gen. Sir Charles Ronald Llewelyn Guthrie, GCB, LVO, OBE
2 Dec 1991	Lt-Gen. Sir Jeremy John George Mackenzie, KCB, OBE
31 Aug 1992	1 (BR) Corps disbanded and position abolished

The Allied Command Europe Rapid Reaction Corps (ARRC) was established using 1 (BR) Corps headquarters as its basis; the last commander of 1 (BR) Corps became its first commander, and it has continued to have a British lieutenant general in command.

1 Oct 1992	Lt-Gen. Sir Jeremy John George Mackenzie, KCB, OBE
8 Dec 1994	Lt-Gen. Sir Michael John Dawson Walker, GCB, CMG, CBE
13 Jan 1997	Lt-Gen. Sir Michael (Mike) David Jackson, KCB, CBE, DSO
26 Jan 2000	Lt-Gen. Christopher Francis Drewry, CBE
15 Jan 2003	Lt-Gen. Sir (Francis) Richard Dannatt, KCB, CBE, MC
19 Jan 2005	Lt-Gen David Richards, CBE, DSO

---

[260] Stockwell transferred Aug 1956 to II Corps, established for the Suez operation that fall, and returned ca. Nov 1956.

Principal Garrison Cities in Germany

This table lists all cities containing headquarters for brigades and larger formations.

City	Formations
Bad Lippspringe	33rd Armoured Brigade 1950—1956
	11th Infantry Brigade 1961—1964
Bad Oyenhausen	BAOR 1948—1954
	1 Corps 1951—1953
Bielefeld	1 Corps 1953—1992
Bunde	6th Armoured Division 1953—1958
Delmenhorst	5th AGRA (AA) 1950—1958
Detmold	20th Armoured Brigade 1957—1977
	TF Hotel 1977—1980
	20th Armoured Brigade 1981—1992
Dortmund	7th Artillery Brigade (AA) 1961—1977
	1st Artillery Division 1977—1980
	Artillery Division 1980—1984
	1st Artillery Brigade 1985—1993
Gütersloh[261]	7th Artillery Brigade (AA) briefly 1961
	102nd Logistic Brigade 1999 to date
Herford	11th Armoured Division 1951—1956
	6th Armoured Division 1951—1953
	4th Infantry Division 1956—1958
	4th Division 1958—1977
	4th Armoured Division 1977—1993
	1st (UK) Armoured Division 1993 to date
Hilden	2nd Infantry Division 1947—1958
	2nd Division 1958—1961
Hildesheim	91st Lorried Infantry Brigade 1951—1956
	10th Infantry Brigade 1956—1957
	12th Infantry Brigade 1957
	1st Artillery Brigade 1961—1977
Hohne	TF Bravo 1977—1980
	22nd Armoured Brigade 1981—1993
	7th Armoured Brigade 1993 to date
Hubblerath	4th Infantry [later Guards] Brigade 1947—1964
Iserlohn	5th Infantry Brigade 1947—1964
	4th Guards Brigade 1964—1968

---

[261] Until 1994, a major RAF base.

City	Formations
Lubbecke	2nd Division 1961—1976

City	Formations
Lubbecke	2nd Division 1961—1976
	2nd Armoured Division 1976—1982
Luneburg	31st Lorried Infantry Brigade 1951—1956
	10th Infantry Brigade 1957—1958
Minden	31st Lorried Infantry Brigade1951
	61st Lorried Infantry Brigade 1952—1956
	11th Infantry Brigade 1956—1961
	11th Infantry Brigade 1964—1970
	11th Armoured Brigade 1970—1977
	TF Golf 1977—1980
	11th Armoured Brigade 1981—1993
Munster	6th Infantry Brigade 1947—1951
	20th Armoured Brigade 1952—1956
	6th Infantry Brigade 1956—1957
	6th Infantry Brigade 1958—1968[262]
	4th Guards Brigade 1968—1970
	4th Armoured Brigade 1970—1976
	TF Charlie 1976—1980
	4th Armoured Brigade 1981—1993
Osnabrück	31st Lorried Infantry Brigade 1947—1950
	12th Infantry Brigade 1956—1957
	21st Infantry Brigade 1956—1958
	12th Infantry Brigade 1958—1970
	12th Mechanised Brigade 1970—1976
	TF Delta 1976—1980
	5th Field Force 1977—1981
	12th Armoured Brigade 1981—1993
	4th Armoured Brigade 1993 to date
Paderborn	TF Echo 1977—1980
	33rd Armoured Brigade 1981—1992
	20th Armoured Brigade 1992—1999
Rheindahlen	BAOR 1954—1994
	ARRC 1992 to date
	1st (UK) Signal Brigade 1995 to date
Sennelager	20th Armoured Brigade 1999 to date

---

[262] 6th Infantry Brigade was withdrawn to the UK in 1968, but still assigned to BAOR.

City	Formations
Soest	6th Armoured Brigade 1971—1977
	TF Foxtrot 1977—1980
	3rd Armoured Division 1978—1993
	6th Armoured Brigade 1981—1984
	6th Airmobile Brigade 1984—1987
	6th Armoured Brigade 1988—1993
Soltau	7th Armoured Brigade 1947—1956
	7th Armoured Brigade 1957—1977
	TF Alpha 1977—1980
	7th Armoured Brigade 1981—1993
Verden	7th Armoured Division 1947—1958
	5th Division 1958—1960
	1st Division 1960—1977
	1st Armoured Division 1977—1992
Wuppertal	6th Infantry Brigade 1951—1956
	6th Infantry Brigade 1957—1958

Formation Signs

Re-introduced during World War II, formation signs continued through the 1950s. They largely disappeared after 1960 with the demise of battledress. At that point, they were little-seen except on bulletin boards or unit stationary. However, they did linger, and by the 1990s formation signs were again regularly worn on uniforms.

British Army of the Rhine

BAOR retained the formation sign of 21st Army Group: two Crusader's swords in gold, crossed with points downwards, on a blue cross on a red shield. NATO's HQ Northern Army Group (NORTHAG) had its own formation sign: a yellow axe on a blue shield on a blue-black rectangle.

Rhine Army Troops had a single sword, point downwards, on reversed colors: red cross on a blue shield.

The basic BAOR blue cross on a red shield was the starting point for any number of formation signs. Rhine Army Training Centre had a gold torch of learning superimposed. The BAOR RAC Training Centre had a white tank (similar to that worn by the Royal Tank Regt) on crossed white lances. The BAOR School of Artillery added the antique cannon of the RA badge in gold below "S of A" also in gold (with the letters on the cross-arms). Finally, the BAOR Engineer Training Establishment had the RE badge in gold (flaming grenade above scroll with "UBIQUE").

Two districts, Hamburg and Hanover, also had formation signs. The former had a blue cross on a yellow shield. The latter had a rearing white horse on a red shield. The Hamburg District formation sign was also used by Rhine District.

1 Corps

1 Corps also retained its wartime sign: a spearhead in white on an elongated red diamond. When the corps was disbanded, a variant of the spearhead was utilized by the new Allied Rapid Reaction Corps (ARRC) for its sign. During World War II, 1 Corps Artillery had the spearhead on an elongated diamond divided vertically (blue left and red right), while 1 Corps Troops RE added to two diagonal stripes to the normal red diamond. These formation signs may have been revived in 1951 when the corps reformed.

Divisions and Brigades

1st Division retained the old 1st Infantry Division sign: a white triangle. Headquarters wore it with a thin red border. RA, Royal Signals, and RASC units in 1st Division wore the white triangle, but on elongated diamond: divided vertically red and blue for RA, all blue for Royal Signals, and blue and yellow for RASC. After this formation became 1st Armoured Division in the late 1970s, it took a new sign: a charging rhinoceros in white on a black triangle trimmed in red. This harked back to the sign of the World War II 1st Armoured Division while retaining the triangular shape of 1st Infantry Division.

2nd Infantry Division, later 2nd Division and 2nd Armoured Division, and then 2nd Infantry Division again, used throughout its World War II sign: white crossed keys on a black rectangle or square.

3rd Armoured Division kept the old 3rd Infantry Division sign: a red equilateral triangle, point downwards, on a black equilateral triangle.

4th Division had a red circle with the fourth quadrant displaced. This could be worn on a white square (2nd pattern) or black square (3rd pattern).

5th Division used a white "Y" on a black circle (a variant of its World War II sign).

6th Armoured Division readopted its World War II sign: a white mailed fist on a black square. This was later adopted by 20th Armoured Brigade, which changed the square to blue.

7th Armoured Division had a red jerboa (desert rat), outlined in white, on a black rectangle. This was later taken over for use by 7th Armoured Brigade, which changed thebackground to a white square or rectangle.

11th Armoured Division had a black bull, with details (face, horns, and hooves) in red, on a yellow rectangle.

4th Guards Brigade used the World War II sign of the Guards Armoured Division (white eye on blue shield trimmed in red) with a white "IV" below the eye.

4th Armoured Brigade re-adopted the World War II sign of black Jerboa (desert rat) on a white square. (The jerboa was in a different pose than for the 7th.)

5th and 6th Infantry Brigades adopted similar designs: crossed bayonet and key in white on a square with the numeral "5" or "6" above (the key linking them to the 2nd Infantry Division formation sign). For 5th Infantry Brigade, the square was red and the numeral blue; for 6th Infantry Brigade the square was blue and the numeral red.

15th (North East) Infantry Brigade had a Merlin [small bird of prey] in natural colors on a burgundy rectangle.

19th Infantry Brigade wore a red triangle containing a black panther's head with a yellow (or gold) tongue and eyes.

24th Infantry Brigade retained the World War II sign of 24th Guards Brigade, an heraldic wing in the form of a crest in red on a dark blue rectangle.

49th (East) Infantry Brigade adopted the old sign of the 49th (West Riding) Infantry Division: a white polar bear on an ice floe, all on a black rectangle.

Artillery

1st AGRA used a white ram's head with black markings on a red square. 5th AGRA (AA) used a an arrow in red with a wheel device in the center, on a blue square. 7th AGRA (AA) had a yellow Centaur and bow on a dark blue square.

Guided weapons regiments wore a diamond divided vertically (red left and blue right) with a yellow missile in the center pointing upwards.

Berlin

British Troops in Berlin originally used a red ring on a black disc. This was later changed to a red circle, with the letters "BERLIN" above, also in red, all on a black rectangle. This has also been shown as a circle with connected tab on tap.

Signals

1st (UK) Signal Brigade uses a white spearhead on an elongated blue diamond. This was the old formation sign for 1 Corps Signals, and may have been used by them while 1 Corps was active.

Appendix: The Original British Army of the Rhine

When British Army of the Rhine (BAOR) was formed in Mar 1919, it had a cavalry division and five corps, each with two infantry divisions:

II Corps: Southern and Light Divisions (ex 29th and 2nd)
IV Corps: Lowland and Highland Divisions (ex 9th and 62nd)
VI Corps: London and Northern Divisions (ex 41st and 33rd)
IX Corps: Western and Midland Divisions (ex 1st and 6th)
X Corps: Lancashire and Eastern Divisions (ex 32nd and 34th)

The Lowland, Highland, Western, Midland and Eastern Divisions lasted only until Aug 1919, when they were disbanded. The remaining five were disbanded in Nov 1919. Troops in the Rhineland were then grouped as The Independent Division; there were also troops in eastern Germany known as the Upper Silesia Force.

While New Armies and TF battalions survived into 1919 as part of BAOR, the divisions appear to have been reinforced or continued with a large number of former training battalions.[263] Twenty-three of these battalions were absorbed into other battalions of their regiments between Feb and Jun 1919. Two other battalions were simply disbanded on the Rhine in Apr 1919. Six more of these battalions were disbanded Oct and Nov 1919, as BAOR eliminated the remainder of its original divisions. However, the last of these battalions did not disappear until the next year; five were disbanded on the Rhine in Feb and five more in Mar 1920.

By 1920, The Independent Division was gone[264] and the force in Germany comprised the Rhine Brigade and the Upper Silesia Force (two brigades):

Rhine Brigade — 1st Bn R Irish Regt, 4th Bn Worcesters, 2nd Bn Black Watch, 1st and 3rd Bns Middlesex Regt, 1st Bn Durham LI
1st Silesia Brigade — 2nd Bn R Inniskilling Fusiliers, 2nd Bn Leinster Regt
2nd Silesia Brigade — 2nd Bn Connaught Rangers, 1st Bn R Munster Fusiliers

---

[263] In autumn 1917, most surviving battalions from the Training Reserve were affiliated to regiments in groups of three, as the 51st and 52nd (Graduated) Bns and 53rd (Young Soldiers) Bn. In Feb 1919, all of those active were redesignated as (Service) battalions.
[264] Feb or Mar 1920 seems a likely date, as the last ten of the 50-series battalions were disbanded in Germany that month. Given "the Troubles" in Ireland, the large number of (mainly southern) Irish battalions in Germany is probably not a coincidence.

From 1922, BAOR comprised two Rhine brigades, which survived into 1929 when BAOR was disbanded and the British withdrew.[265]

1st Rhine Brigade

1st Bn Northumberland Fus	1922 – 1926
1st Bn W Yorkshire Regt	1922 – 1926
2nd Bn QO Cameron Highlanders	1922 – 1926
1st Bn York & Lancaster Regt	1922 – 1924
2nd Bn R Berkshire Regt	1926 – 1928
2nd Bn R Welch Fusiliers	1926 – 1929
2nd Bn Worcestershire Regt	1926 – 1928

2nd Rhine Brigade

2nd Bn Duke of Cornwall's LI	1922 – 1924
1st Bn KO Yorkshire LI	1922 – 1924
2nd Bn KRRC	1922 – 1925
1st Bn Royal Ulster Rifles	1922 – 1926
1st Bn Manchester Regt	1923 – 1924
2nd Bn King's Shropshire LI	1924 – 1927
1st Bn Oxford & Bucks LI	1925 – 1927
2nd Bn Royal Fusiliers	1926 – 1929
2nd Bn Leicestershire Regt	1927 – 1929
2nd Bn Dorsetshire Regt	1928 – 1929

Cavalry, Artillery and Engineers

There was one cavalry regiment present from 1919, 14th King's Hussars. It was amalgamated Oct 1922 at Cologne with the inactive 20th Hussars to form 14th/20th Hussars, and returned to the UK in 1923. 1st King's Dragoon Guards were stationed in Germany 1924—1927 and 8th King's Royal Irish Hussars 1927—1929.

3rd Brigade RFA was in Germany 1920—1923. 8th Brigade RFA came to Germany in 1921 and remained to 1927 [redesignated May 1924 as 8th Field Brigade RA]. The last artillery unit was 19th Field Brigade RA 1927—1929.

7th Field Company RE served in Germany 1919—1929.

---

[265] The following battalions served in BAOR during the periods indicated, but brigade allocation is not known: 1st Bn Duke of Wellington's (1922-23), 2nd Bn Hampshire (1928-29), and 1st Bn South Lancs (1928-29).

Glossary and Abbreviations

This does not include shortened forms of regimental titles, which should all be understandable.

Abbott	105mm SP Gun (FV433) which entered service in 1965; replaced in the early 1990s by the AS90.
AGRA	Army Group Royal Artillery: a headquarters for GHQ artillery regiments, designated (Field) or (Anti-Aircraft) depending on composition. In 1961 these were redesignated brigades.
APC	Armoured Personnel Carrier (wheeled or tracked vehicle for infantry transport or a myriad of other uses); in many armies infantry replaced APCs with infantry fighting vehicles (IFVs) or mechanised combat vehicles (MCVs) intended for combat as well as transport); see Warrior.
ARRC	Allied Command Europe Rapid Reaction Corps, formed in 1992 as a standing corps headquarters (at Bielefeld) to be prepared to deploy under NATO or other auspices to a designated area, to undertake combined and joint operations. Six divisions—including 1st (UK) Armoured Division—and corps troops are designated for possible operational assignment. Based initially on 1 Corps and always commanded by a British general.
AS90	155mm SP Gun introduced 1993, replacing the M109 and the Abbott.
ATGW	Anti-Tank Guided Weapon (sometimes, ATGM for Anti-Tank Guided Missile). The two main versions used in the British Army are Swingfire (mounted on vehicles and helicopters) and Milan (vehicle-mounted or man portable).
AVRE	Armoured Vehicle RE: designed for breaching minefields, crossing gaps, and clearing obstacles. These are all built on a tank chassis, using successively the Centurion (from the 1950s, replacing World War II versions) and the Chieftain.
Centurion	Main battle tank (MBT) developed at the end of World War II and in production through 1962.
Challenger	MBT; Challenger 1 was delivered between 1983 and 1990. Challenger 2 delivered between 1994 and 2000 and is the current MBT for the British Army.
Chieftain	MBT produced in the 1970s to replace the Centurion, and itself replaced by the Challenger.

Conqueror   A heavy tank in service between 1954 and the 1960s; the first to mount a 120mm gun.

Corporal   An early US surface to surface missile used by two regiments from ca. 1959 to 1967. The British did not acquire the US followup missile, the Sergeant.

CS   Close support [US direct support]: tasked for support of a specific formation (generally a brigade).

EW   Electronic Warfare (specialized signals role involving the interception, analysis, and jamming of electronic communications).

FH70   Towed 155mm howitzer developed by Germany, Italy and the UK and introduced ca. 1979.

FV432   First tracked APC introduced into the British Army (delivered between 1963 and 1972), with many variants; as a basic APC was restricted to battalions in Germany.

FV438   Variant of the FV432 with Swingfire ATGW, found at first in armoured regiments, and then for a time in batteries of the Royal Artillery; it returned to the armoured regiments in the 1980s before being withdrawn from service ca. 1990-1992.

GPMG   General Purpose Machine-Gun

GS   General support (compare with CS—close support).

GW   Guided Weapons; used to indicate an artillery unit equipped with missiles (surface to air or surface to surface), mainly in the 1960s.

Honest John   A 762mm rocket with a nuclear warhead. In service 1960-1976.

Lance   A 557mm battlefield missile with a nuclear warhead. One regiment was equipped with it beginning 1975-77; withdrawn from service in 1993.

M44   US 155mm SP howitzer developed after World War II introduced ca. 1956 and later replaced by Abbott.

M107   US 175mm SP gun used by "depth fire" regiments.

M109   US 155mm SP howitzer, taken into service ca. late 1960s.

M110   US 8" (203mm) SP howitzer introduced in the 1960s and withdrawn from service in the early1990s.

M115   US towed 8" (203mm) howitzer developed in World War II and continued un use until replaced by the SP M110.

MLRS   227mm Multiple Launched Rocket System, on a fully-tracked vehicle, introduced with heavy regiments to replace the M107 gun in the depth fire role.

NAAFI   Navy, Army and Air Force Institutes. Official trading organization to the British Armed Forces, providing retail and

	leisure services to military personnel and their families.
Phoenix	An unmanned air vehicle: a surveillance and target acquisition drone.
Rapier	Low level air defence weapon. First regiments converted by 1973. Vehicle mounted or towed mount.
recce	Reconnaissance; in the early years recce regiments were actually just armoured car regiments, until the "combat vehicle reconnaissance (tracked)" family was introduced in 1972 and the regiments became all-tracked. Among the variants, the Scimitar remained in service until replaced by the Sabre (created from a Scimitar body and Fox armoured car turret); the ATGW, command, APC, and command versions are also still in use (all with unique names). Vehicles derived from this series are used as a mount for the Starstreak HVM SAM and as an engineer vehicle.
roulement	Literally, "rotation" (from the French), the term describing the regular movement of units from one station to another, either on permanent or short-term assignment.
Saladin	A 6x6 armoured car (FV601) in production 1959 to 1972 and replaced by tracked armoured recce vehicles.
SAM	Surface to air missile. Man portable versions are the Blowpipe (entered service 1972), Javelin (entered service ca. late 1980s), and Starstreak HVM [high velocity missile] (entered service ca. 1992). See also Rapier and Thunderbird.
Saracen	6x6 wheeled APC (FV603) in production from 1953 to 1972; used in armoured car regiments and then mechanised battalions in Germany, where it was at first manned by personnel from armoured regiments until the infantry assumed responsibility for crewing them in 1963.
Saxon	Wheeled 4x4 APC (AT-105) taken into service 1983 for UK-based mechanised battalions.
Sexton	World War II SP 25-pounder.
SSM	Surface to surface missile.
Thunderbird	One of two British medium- or higher-level SAMs, which equipped two regiments in Germany (withdrawn 1977).
u/c	under the control of.
Warrior	Mechanized combat vehicle—later termed infantry combat vehicle or infantry fighting vehicle (FV510) introduced beginning in 1986 to replace the FV432 APC. Until the 1992 Options for Change it was only issued to mechanised battalions in Germany.

Sources

As expressed in the Preface, both authors are indebted to the information and leads provided (in alphabetical order) by Messrs. Ewen Bayley, Mike Cox, Geoff Fletcher, and Dave Leftwich. Mr. Fletcher also provided a draft of his article on 3rd Infantry Division 1959-1977. In addition to the material assembled by Dr Watson and assistance from these four, the following sources were used.

Bainton, Roy. *The Long Patrol: The British in Germany Since 1945*. (Edinburgh and London: Mainstream Publishing, 2003)

Bellis, Malcolm A. *The British Army Overseas, 1945—1970*. (Published 2001 by Malcolm A. Bellis.)

Blaxland, Gregory. *The Regiments Depart: A History of the British Army, 1945-1970*. (London: William Kimber & Co., Ltd, 1971)

The British Army: A Pocket Guide [1992 edition] (Shrewsbury: Royal&F [Military Publishing] 1991)

Davis, Brian L. *British Army Cloth Insignia 1940 to the Present: An Illustrated Reference Guide for Collectors*. (London: Arms and Armour Press, 1985)

"4 CMBG" *Army, Maple Leaf*, 15 September 2004, Vol. 7 No. 30, online at http://www.forces.gc.ca/site/community/mapleleaf/html_files/ html_view_e.asp?page=vol7-30army

Frederick, J. B. M. *Lineage Book of British Land Forces 1660-1978*. (2 vols) (Wakefield, Yorks: Microform Academic Publishers, 1984)

Heyman, Charles. *The British Army Pocket Guide 1997/1998*. (Barnsley: Pen & Sword Books Ltd, 1997) and *The British Army Pocket Guide 2000-2001* (Barnsley: Pen & Sword Books Ltd, 2000)

Historical Section, Canadian Army. Army Headquarters Report No. 51, The 27th Canadian Infantry Brigade Group February 1951 - May 1952 (6 May 1952).

The History and Traditions of The Royal Scots Dragoon Guards (Carabiniers and Greys). (Aldershot: The Forces Press, n.d. [ca. 1971])

Lord, Cliff. Unpublished histories of 2nd Infantry Division and 5th Infantry Brigade.

Lord, Cliff and Graham Watson. *The Royal Corps of Signals: Unit Histories of the Corps (1920—2001) and its Antecedents.* (Solihull, West Midlands: Helion and Company Ltd, 2003)

Mackinlay, Gordon Angus. "British Mechanised Infantry: How It Started." Posting (1 Jan 2002) to British Regiments online group [britregiments@yahoo.com].

Macksey, Kenneth. *The Tanks: The History of the Royal Tank Regiment, 1945-1975.* (London: Arms and Armour Press, 1979)

Messenger, Charles. *For Love of Regiment. A History of British Infantry.* Vol 2: 1915-1994. (London: Leo Cooper, 1996)

MicroMark. List B39M: British 24th Air Mobile Brigade 1989-1993.
MicroMark. List B41M: British Berlin Garrison 1986-1994.
MicroMark. List B51M: British Armoured Division 1965-1972.
MicroMark. List B52M: British Infantry Brigade 1964-1972.
MicroMark. ListB58M: British Territorial Army 1995+.
MicroMark. List B60M: British Armoured Division 1986-1990.
MicroMark. List B61M: British BAOR Corps Support 1986-1990.
MicroMark. List B63M: British 24th Air Mobile Brigade 1993-1999.
[The MicroMark lists were apparently designed for wargamers and carry no publication date (or even the name "MicroMark") on them. In at least some cases the publication was late in 1999, since B55M notes that 5th Airborne Brigade "was disbanded" in Sep 1999 on formation of the new 16th Air Assault Brigade. These sheets contain fairly detailed TOE information as well as some general organizational and order of battle details.]

Mileham, Patrick. "Fifty Years of British Army Officership 1960—2010." "Part I: Retrospective" in *Defense & Security Analysis* Mar 2004 (Vol 20, No 1), 69-86, and "Part II: Prospective" in *Defense & Security Analysis* Jun 2004 (Vol 20, No 2), 179-199.

Mills, T. F. Notes on modern British formations collected by Mr. Mills and generously provided. Also, the UK portion of his site "Land Forces of Britain, the Empire, and the Commonwealth": http://regiments.org/

Ministry of Defence. *Operations in Iraq: First Reflections.* (July 2003)

Pimlot, John (ed.). *British Military Operations 1945-1984.* (New York: The Military Press, 1984)

"RE 200" brochure published 1987 on the history of the Royal Engineers; located at http://www.royal-engineers.co.uk/pages/brochure/re2_frames.html [an unofficial web site on the RE]

Rosignoli, Guido. *Army Badges and Insignia since 1945, Book One.* (New York: Macmillan Publishing Co., Inc., 1973)

Rottman, Gordon. *Armies of the Gulf War.* Osprey Elite Series No. 45. (London: Osprey Publishing Ltd, 1993)

Schülze, Carl. *The British Army of the Rhine.* Europa/Military No. 19 (London: Windrow & Greene Ltd, 1995)

Schülze, Carl. *British 24 Airmobile Brigade.* Europa/Military No. 23 (Ramsbury, Wilts: The Crowod Press, 1999)

Web sites
Allied Rapid Reaction Corps, www.arrc.nato.int/
British Army, www.army.mod.uk/army/
another site is www.armedforces.co.uk/army/listings
British Forces Germany, bfgnet.de/bfgnet/home/homesub/home.htm
The British Army, http://www.armedforces.co.uk/armyindex.htm
Royal Regiment of Artillery Information, www.wohnungssuche.com/
        Raa/info/main.htm
36th Heavy Air Defence Regt RA, http://members.tripod.com/krh30/
        36reg/id26.htm

There is a British Army of the Rhine website, created by a private individual and last updated in Jul 2004: http://baor.homestead.com/BAORindex20.html. This is of limited use to the orbat enthusiast, but still generates some message traffic from those seeking fellow members of their units. Roy Bainton used the site to search for individuals willing to be interviewed for his *Long Patrol* book.

Index of Formations

This index is limited to divisions and brigades. Redesignations over the years meant that the same unit could have several different designations (e.g., 2nd Infantry Division became 2nd Division, then 2nd Armoured Division, and then 2nd Infantry Division again; 4th Infantry Brigade became 4th Guards Brigade and then 4th Armoured Brigade). Because of this, entries in the index have not been grouped, but each formation listed under whatever designation it had on the indicated page. Divisions and brigades from the Appendix on the original BAOR are not included in this Index.

Lightning Source UK Ltd.
Milton Keynes UK
UKHW030610071119
353079UK00006B/537/P